Dy

Communi

MW01181863

Effective Keys to Preventing Relationship Breakdowns -
Enjoying the Benefits of Maintaining a Healthy Sex
Life in your Marriage

James Olah

The Dynamics of Communication and Sex:
Effective Keys to Preventing Relationship Breakdowns - Enjoying the Benefits of Maintaining a Healthy Sex Life in your Marriage

Improving Your Relationship Series: Book 2

First Edition January 2012
Second Edition February 2012
Third Edition November 2013 – Revision

ISBN-13: 978-1494238346
ISBN-10: 1494238349

SOJO Books
Published by Amazon Kindle Books

Table of Contents

Dedication

I want to thank some of the people who have encouraged me and helped me on this project.

My friend Irv Holtzhouse just finished his degree to become a counselor and he gave me insight that was developed in chapter four on the brain. That was an area of consideration that didn't cross my mind when I first started developing the book.

My daughter Heather has always been a person I could bounce ideas off and she would give me honest responses. Sometimes she tells me what might sound like I was going too far or off base when dealing with certain topics. She also encourages when something is right-on as well. She also helped with the grammar and picking up on spelling errors that spell check didn't catch.

My niece Melissa did a final grammar check. It's so nice having people in the family who will take the time to help out on a project like this.

Finally I want to thank my wife Nancy for her ideas, thoughts and evaluation of the book she listened to me talk about my perspectives and ideas concerning this book and gave me valuable insights from a feminine perspective. Many of the thoughts I share with you in this book are insights I've learned in our relationship, and they were not always easy for either of us to learn at the time. She has always been an encourager and the cheer leader I needed to stay focused.

Just before I published this book it was found that my wife has cancer. I am finding that the teachings I have put together in this book about the importance of listening and engaging in conversation are not just invaluable but also very enjoyable as we talk about concerns and face end of life issues. Our level of communication we learned is allowing us to be very open and forthright in expressing our love, concern, fear and hope in a difficult time. We experienced closeness during that time that went well beyond our expectations. See "My Story" in chapter four for more details.

Introduction

Every couple faces battles in their relationship which stem from them not understanding the greatest need and motivation of the other. We often think that the person ought to just understand us or "get it" after a while. But when they don't we think they are out to get us, or don't truly care about us or worse yet seek to purposely offend us. That is where disappointment starts and the hurts begin, the battle line drawn and eventually the disagreements start. Fights don't usually happen instantly, but are often born out of a slow burn until unpleasant words become more frequent. If you are passive aggressive it will be more of a quiet struggle, but the hurt feelings are just as real, for they are now underground rather than out in the open to properly address.

When a child is whiney at the end of a long day at Disney you know it is because they are tired and have expended their energy. They are on overload and don't know how to handle it. You can't reason your child out of their irritable state. They just need sleep. You are patient with them because you understand their needs. We are willing to be patient with our children, but why are we so unwilling to respond to the needs of our spouse with the same kind of patient understanding? The purpose of this book is to help you appreciate the motivation of your mate. When you do understand their motivation you can be more patient with them and seek to work with them more effectively.

Why does she have to talk and give every detail of what went on in the day? Why does he come home and reveal nothing or very little of what went on in his day but instead just wants to sit around and do nothing or go out and play sports or work in the garage? Do you know what motivates a woman to ask all those questions? Do you know her deepest need? Do you know of the loneliness in her soul? Do you know why he doesn't think it is so important to connect with you by sharing the details of his day?

Why does he seem to have only one thing on his mind? How can we have a disagreement and then after we have sex he thinks everything is all right and settled? Do you understand those deep needs of a man and why he functions like he does? He may not even understand why sex is so important to him either.

1

This book seeks to help you understand what motivates your mate so you can better understand them and therefore respond in appropriate ways. Also, this may give you insight as to why you are motivated to do what you do. With understanding comes the potential for change as well as the enrichment of your relationship. Without understanding you will continue to do the same old thing and be frustrated in your relationship. Will you choose continual frustration or decide to pursue enrichment?

As you read this book you will find yourself saying "my partner needs to read this because now I understand why I feel or act that way. I just haven't been able to articulate the importance of my needs clearly before. I want them to understand me better." The more we understand our own needs and how they fulfill us when they are met, the easier it is to understand the needs of our mate and, therefore, to value them.

The title I've chosen for this book is "The Dynamics of Communication and Sex". The word Dynamic means *"Change producing force: the forces that tend to produce activity and change in any situation or sphere of existence"*. The content of this book helps you focus your understanding on the dynamics of sex and communication in your relationship.

After one of my editing sessions in reworking this manuscript I was taking a trip with my wife and I said, "I wish we had a book like this available when we first got married for it would have given us better understanding of each other and helped us avoid a lot of mistakes." It is my desire that this book can help you avoid common pitfalls and deepen your relationship. Enjoy the journey!

The Dynamics of Communication and Sex

Most couples remember a time when they couldn't get enough of each other. They would talk for hours on end. He wouldn't want to leave when he dropped her off after a date, and they would just talk about everything. Now she asks, "Why doesn't he talk to me? We used to talk for hours when we were dating and I knew everything about him but now I can't get him to open up with me and share any of his dreams and concerns and worst of all he doesn't seem to care what's going on in my life."

That is not the only thing that has changed in the relationship. He remembers the passion they used to have together when they were playful and couldn't keep their hands off each other. Now he asks, "Why doesn't she want to have sex with me very much? She used to be so full of passion, and now she is stoic when I make advances or touch her and she makes a joke when I bring up us being together intimately". Have you contemplated anything like that about your relationship? Have you wondered where the spark went? Is there a possibility of reigniting it again? Why did it desert your relationship?

Even though there is much more to marriage than conversation and sex, these are important elements to a good marriage. So, what does communication and sex have in common? To understand this, one must understand what each of these accomplishes for both the man and woman.

When it comes to sex, it has been said that women are like crock-pots and men are like microwave ovens. Men are ready to engage at a moment's notice. Women need time to be wooed. Good communication and having her emotional needs met is foreplay for the woman. [1]Many sex therapists say that, for women, foreplay is everything that happens in the twenty four hours preceding sex. For her it starts in the mind and needs to be nourished. In studies it is found that women think about sex about every other day. Men, however think about sex every other minute. All it takes for men to get ready is visual stimulation, thoughts and touch, and not always very much of it, and he is ready to engage sex right now. The differences are obvious and often joked about. However the seriousness of communication and sex is no joking matter.

So, what is it that communication and sex have in common? You might think it is complicated psychology, but as you think about your relationship it becomes quite obvious. The answer is, they both accomplish the same kind of fulfillment in a man's and woman's inner being. Does that have your curiosity piqued? I hope so, because it is imperative that both understand what each act accomplishes for the other.

Let me introduce Edward and Susan

As I was writing this book I found that it was confusing at times to talk about the man and woman, he and she, him and her. Sometimes it seemed difficult to follow. If I got confused then it stands to reason it would be harder for you to follow as well. So I invited a couple to join us for the "him and her, or he and she" part in this book. Edward James is taking the he parts and Susan Beth is taking the she parts of this book. Ed was named after both his grandfathers. Sue was named after her mother's best friend and favorite aunt. Ed came from a strong family. Sue came from a single parent home where her grandfather provided a good male role model for her in the absence of a father, but she never saw how male/female marriage interaction worked in her own family setting.

They met in college at a basketball game during their junior year and she caught his eye and before they knew it they were dating regularly. Right after college they both got good jobs and six months later they got married. During the three years of their marriage they have had their ups and downs but they are still getting to understand each other along with the differences between the male and female roles and how they need to interact. Both are committed to making their marriage work and grow through reading and discussion. Neither is afraid to express their mind when they don't agree. They have been together long enough to know that there is a lot more to learn about understanding their relationship as well as what drives them in it.

Just so you know, when I talk about Ed I am talking about men in general. When I talk about Sue I am talking about women in general. Bringing them into the book has helped make the book clearer and perhaps a little more personal. When talking about communication and sex, there are few hard and fast rules that apply to every person. Take what applies to you, and make your relationship better as well as your understanding of the other more clear. Look forward to your great adventure of discovery as a couple. For some it will be an unfamiliar and uncomfortable journey, but the destination is well worth the cost and investment of your life.

Chapter One: Women and Communication

Most women enjoy talking. I heard a story of a teen girl who was on a missionary trip. They had traveled all day and it was late at night that they got on a bus to finish the last few hours of their trip. This girl was talking nonstop to her seat mate. Finally the seat mate fell asleep. When the talking girl noticed her friend was asleep she turned to look out the window and upon seeing her reflection continued talking. Why is the need that strong for some women to talk so much? Even though most women are not like that girl, it doesn't diminish the powerful need of women to engage in meaningful conversation as a regular and needful part of their life.

Sue is about relationship. She wants to cultivate and nurture her connection with Ed. This is Sue's motivation behind talking. Communication is about passing on information that builds connection by being understood and feeling a part of the other's life. When Sue speaks to Ed, it is with the intention of wanting to feel connected by learning more about what is going on inside of his mind and understanding what happened in his day. Through communication she is seeking to build their bond and thus, allay her fear of isolation. That is why, when Ed comes home, Sue wants to share the experiences of her day. She wants him to care and learn more about what she has experienced that day when she details what went on. It is in this way that Sue seeks for Ed to connect with her. She will share not only what happened but also express her opinions, observations and feelings, both negative and positive, about what happened. Sue will then turn to Ed and want to find out such details about his day.

Ed, like most men, can sometimes become annoyed with Susan's trivial information and explicated details at times, because he doesn't understand why she is telling him every aspect of what went on in her day. Sue's motivation is that the more Ed knows about her, the better he can understand her and the greater will be his connection with her. However, Ed may view all that detail as overwhelming or that she is talking for the sake of talking and it may even seem inconsequential or non-sense to him. Why talk about it in such length!? Why does the story need so much detail Sue? He fails to realize that when Susan talks about those details that this is the way women observe all of life. To not allow her to share these thoughts leads to frustration on her part, because she thinks Ed is not interested in her. Sue then reasons, "How can Ed be close to me if he is not interested in what happens in my life?"

When Ed is away from Susan she may experience a stronger sense of isolation and the way she combats isolation is to share the details of what happened during his absence. Her motivation is that when she fills him in on the details of her day it brings him back into her life and now they can both feel more connected. Does Sue understand the "why" of what she is doing? Sue happened to know exactly why she was sharing such detail. That is not necessarily true with all women; they just know they need to share what went on in their day. Ed, like most men, does not understand why women need the depth of communication with which he does not feel comfortable. You can go one step further and also recognize that most men don't know the "why" of his intense need for sex. Ed and Sue both just know what they need to feel secure and fulfilled in the relationship. They don't always understand why.

When Sue shares the details of her day, in her mind she feels she has connected with Ed. Now she wants Ed to connect with her? So she asks "what happened in your day Ed?" She is looking for the significant details of Ed's day so she can understand what he went through and how he felt. Ed, like most men doesn't feel he needs to talk about all those details. Fact of the matter is he hasn't learned how to share the kind of details Sue seeks. If he knew why it was important he might take a stab at it more often.

If Ed wants to learn how to meet this need in Sue's life he needs to learn how to share details. Ed comes home day after day and shares nothing with Sue, and what he doesn't realize is that Sue is becoming emptier in her soul every day because he is not connecting with her. He doesn't realize that her need for communication comes from an intense loneliness that she feels. When he minimizes her need to be connected through communication then that loneliness gets more intense. He has the key to break her out of that room of isolation and loneliness, but he doesn't realize that his willingness to communicate is that key that he is withholding from her. He may tend to think such talk and information is worthless, but the reality is that for Sue it is her lifeline to relationship, and her escape from loneliness, it's her connection with her man. (Read that again so you don't miss this important point men!)

Why does Ed think it is not important to share? He thinks it is no big deal to share the details of the day for it really accomplishes nothing, or at least very little. As Ed thinks about this point he comes up with his "man wisdom". If he worked through a problem at his job or with a person at work and brought it to resolution, he is finished with it. It is over. What good does it do to rehash it when it will accomplish nothing? Ed doesn't understand why it is so important for Sue to know the details of what happened and how Ed handled the situation or what he thought and how he responded. He doesn't see the relationship-building aspect of such communication. He doesn't comprehend how it will help Sue feel connected to him.

Because Ed can compartmentalize his life, he can leave his problems at work, realizing that when he is home he doesn't have to talk or think about those problems until the next day. So why talk about it and disturb home time? He doesn't "get it" that such detail helps Sue connect with him and feel a part of his life. Such conversation fulfills an important need within her life for bonding and strengthening relationship and feeling attached to Ed. He may also justify his lack of communication by saying that he doesn't want to over-burden her with problems because Sue tends to worry.

On another front, Ed will get frustrated when Sue asks "why are you so late", or "why didn't you call?" Sue wants to know what tied Ed up or if he had any problems. In a coded way she may be asking "are we having a problem Ed?" Oft times Ed reads this kind of "inquisition" as Sue acting like a parent or being over protective, being a nag, or being on his case. Ed would be surprised to learn that this is not even close to Sue's motivation. She just wants to know what is going on in his life. Remember, for Sue it's all about relationship and connection. You can't have connection if there isn't shared information. Sue wants to know what's been going on so she can be there for Ed, to be a part of his life. Ed has a tendency to misread her concern as a ploy to control him rather than a means for connection and showing love. Ed, in seeking to understand his motivation asked Sue's opinion. "Do you think a lot of men react to their wives like I do because that is the way they responded to their *parents when they were younger?" They feel like they are responding to their parents rather than their spouse. Sue tended to agree with Ed's observation.*

When Ed misread Sue's motivation and responded with snide comments and antagonism, he attacked the core of her being. Sue was confused and became angry with his response because he was thinking the worst of her motivation. So, in order to protect herself from being mistreated, misunderstood or questioned she lashed out at him. If Ed would have decoded Sue's inquiry as an expression of honest concern and truly a means to connect with him, and to be a part of his life, then he would have avoided a great misunderstanding of her motive. He believed a lie rather than seeking out the truth of his wife's intention.

It is important that Ed learns how to decode the intent of Sue's heart. How can he do that? It is really quite easy. When she asks him, "**where have you been**? Or "**Why are you so late**?" (Her tone may sound like she is angry when in reality it is actually frustration and/or fear), it is important that Ed doesn't react to her with his own negative tone. Choose not to respond to anger with anger. Calm yourself. Listen without any thought of defending yourself. Choose the way you are going to respond that says you want to understand her concern. Becoming defensive always hinders the discovery process when a need or concern is expressed. So Ed chooses to be on a mission of discovery rather than setting up a defense with his wife.

The opposite of being defensive is to be open, so Ed needs to listen to Sue and notice how she reacts when he responds calmly to her inquiry. He uses a matter-of-fact tone of voice telling her where he's been or what's happened. Responding with a calm answer can go a long way to soothing her fears and satisfying her questions. Ed often misdiagnosed her expressed concern as criticism of him. Now his eyes were open to other possibilities that helped him to better understand her.

When Ed reacts with a negative tone of voice he realizes that it usually escalates into an argument. Sometimes he takes the coward's way out and reacts with anger or really cutting remarks. He finds such humiliation can control her so she doesn't question him as much. It may quiet her down but he knows it hurts Sue and he often has nagging regrets afterwards. He doesn't know why he reacts that way and he often contemplates how he could respond differently so they could build their relationship rather than experience this tension all the time.

Many arguments that come about when a man is questioned by his wife are because his response is a reaction to her inquiry in which he thinks the worst of her motivation. He thinks she is trying to control him or humiliate him rather than to express concern about him. Have you noticed that most emotional reactions usually lead to argument and conflicts rather than discovery? Be like Spock in Star Trek by logically and objectively looking at her response or her questioning of you. How can you do that? Rather than emotionally reacting right away, take a deep breath, relax and think. Instead of pouncing on her words decide to focus on how you are going to respond in a manner that invokes openness and gentleness. Remember, she is the woman you love. You choose to make her your enemy or friend by the way you respond to what she says.

Putting aside your emotion and really listening to her when you feel you are being attacked tends to take the edge off the situation. Refuse to take it personally so you can better listen to what she has to say. Choose to be calm and concerned in your manner in which you ask for clarification about her concern, for you are seeking to understand her motivation. It is also important that you believe her, because you know her heart. Don't try to defend yourself or offer excuses but listen to what she is saying because that opens you up to better understanding. Reacting always takes you farther away from any kind of solution that will enrich your relationship and bring peace. One other thought. If you have been reacting to her and it has always led to arguments with no resolution, then why not try the method presented above? Good leaders will abandon ways that are not working so they can improve. Are you going to stay in your rut that is destroying your relationship or will you make a new rut going in the direction that will improve your relationship? You have nothing to lose by trying a different method.

Emerson Eggerichs wrote the book "Love and Respect" and talks about the woman's need of unconditional love and the man's need of unconditional respect. I recommend this excellent book that helps you understand the deepest need of each in marriage. In his marriage conference video series he gets to the heart of the issue of what takes us down the wrong track when we typically react rather than respond to what our spouse says: "If you are married to a good willed person, why do you think the worst of them?" That is an expression of 1 Corinthians 13 when Paul describes love as "thinking no evil." It means we don't think the worst of the other.

When wives questions us we immediately think they are attacking us but in reality they are simply making an inquiry. Sometimes the feminine tone of voice which is expressing concern is mistaken for anger as mentioned above. Women are so expressive with their emotions, and their fears cause them to become so animated with various tones that men often misread their real intent. Sue can have tremendous fears that Ed just doesn't understand. When she doesn't know what is happening she fears for him because he is important to her. Her mind immediately imagines the worst. The more insecure she feels the more pronounced her fears are. It is not because Sue doesn't trust Ed (Sometimes men give their wife reason to not trust them because of how they have acted in the past.), but because as a women she tends to be a protector and wants to make sure Ed is all right. Sue shows her love for Ed by being concerned for him. Sometimes Ed can turn that around and think the opposite of her motives. Can you imagine what confusion that causes her?

Our tone of voice in communication can send different messages without our realizing it. You might want to read the author's Kindle book on **Tone of Voice** that explores both the damaging as well as beneficial effects of both feminine and masculine tones.[2]

Let's Talk

When men and women talk, you will often notice two different motivations behind their conversation. When Sue comes to Ed and says, "Let's talk," what's Ed's natural response? They typical male response is: "What do you want to talk about?" Ed is thinking Sue has a specific topic that concerns her. He wants to know what direction the conversation is heading because he is a problem solver and needs facts and information relevant to her concern so he can fix it or make things better. So he thinks the conversation ought to go in a specific direction because she wants to talk. Sue, on the other hand just wants to share information to know what is going on in his or their life. She simply wants to catch up so she can be informed about the concerns of his life. Remember, Sue is relational and needs to talk to connect and wants details of Ed's day both good and bad: what is troubling him, what concerns him, what he is dreaming about and what he fears. When Ed tries to "protect" Sue by not sharing the difficult things with her, he is cutting her out of a very important part of himself that prevents her from being able to connect with him.

When Ed responds to Sue's request to talk and he says "What do you want to talk about"? Sue thinks he ought to just "get it". She "gets it" so why should she have to explain it to Ed? "It's as simple as the nose on your face that I need to be informed about what is going on in your life Ed, you ought to just know that." So with that wrong assumption and not thinking that Ed needs Sue to explain what she needs, the barrier starts to go up between them. This little barrier will lead to a greater barrier that will prevent their relationship from growing.

When Ed engages in conversation with Sue he finds that she will usually talk about people and how things are working out between them. It matters not if Sue spent her day at home or at work, when Ed meets up at the end of the day she will usually focus on people and what's happening in their lives. Sue may talk about how some people can't get along, or didn't get along with her that day. If she took care of the kids she will talk about how they got along and maybe what they did. Sue focuses on the details of what happened, and seeks to understand them relationally. It is important for Ed to take time to notice how Sue focuses on the relational details of what happened in her day. He has learned to ask relevant questions and make appropriate comments about those details as well.

When it comes to what Ed talks about, we find that he is inclined to be a problem solver and he tends to focus on the facts of what happened and how he worked out his problems. Ed loves trivia and statistics. That's one of the draws of sports. It is easier for Ed to describe what happened in his day with bullet points instead of detailed paragraphs. If something was not important he finds no reason to share any details at all with Sue. Ed won't inquire about the personal questions that Sue finds quite natural to seek more information, and she wonders why he didn't know something. Just the other day Ed came home and told Sue that Joe's wife had a baby. In his mind he has shared significant information with her. What more does Sue need to know?

"Was it a boy or girl?" Sue asks.

"I think it was a girl" Ed responds.

"You don't remember what she had?" Sue goes on with her questions. "How long was she? How much did she weigh? What is her name? Did Joe's wife have any problems with the delivery? Is she all right? What hospital was she at? When does she come home from the hospital? Are they going to have a shower for her, or should we just send them a gift? What do you think they need for the baby?"

Ed responds. "I don't know. All I know is that she had a baby and I think it was a girl."

Ed turns and walks away and says "Wow, where did she come up with all those questions? I just made one simple statement and I get the third degree." He was pleased that he was able to report this significant event and thought that he was doing what Sue needed and now she wants all this other information. Ed concludes, "You just can't please women no matter how hard you try! Why do women have to know so much?"

Sue may have left Joe feeling like an idiot because he didn't seek out that important information. She cared about the details, but he didn't. He may have felt humiliated because of the tone of voice she used on him. But that was only an expression of her concern because she had to know. She had no intention to make Joe feel bad in any way.

Those details of the birth were of little concern to Ed. Joe's wife had a baby and that is what was significant. The rest of the details will take care of themselves. Ed doesn't concern himself with the little details that Sue is concerned with knowing. Those details don't come up on Ed's radar so why should he probe for more detail? The less he knows the less he has to remember later to share with Sue and he is alright with that. It's just his perspective that is different than Sue's. She asks all the questions because details are important to her in order to feel connected. Ed should not get upset with her because Sue has this inner craving to know all the details. Such details give the event more meaning and allow her to experience a deeper basis of connection. Sue is also thinking about social obligations for the event like what kind of gift to get, and maybe she is interested in how she can help the mother. Ed hadn't thought about those aspects of Sue's immediate motivation of needing to know all the details.

At the end of the day

Typically, when Sue is sharing the details of what went on during her day she will tend to focus on what happened between people with whom she had contact or talked on the phone or talked about with others. If Sue addresses the frustrations or even the good things of the day, Ed needs to make sure he observes how she usually talks about her feelings. He may notice her anger, joy, frustration, delight, concern or perplexity expressed in her conversation. Details of her conversation will generally focus on how people got along, how they could get along better, how they responded to people or how they acted or should have acted in a certain situation. She generally focuses on the "why" of the details.

However, when Ed talks about what happened in his day he will go over details of how he solved problems, or how someone frustrated him. Typically he will talk about how someone responded to him in a situation, but he is usually less concerned about making relationships right; instead, his concern is that a person is doing what is right. If Ed were involved in sports he would tell Sue the details of the plays, or how Joe had done a lousy job of handling his position. But then again, his wife just had a baby. Ed is concerned with how the game was played and what brought about the win, or who caused the defeat. He generally focuses on the "what" of the details.

The Conversational goal of Women: Reporting/sharing

Sue tends to want to share but not have Ed do problem-solve as a result of her conversation. Sue finds fulfillment in sharing the details of what happened much like a reporter would do. It took a long time for Ed to figure this one out. Sue would tell him about her frustrations at work or with the kids and you can probably guess the course he took with the conversation. He would go into the problem solving mode. He would talk about how she could or should solve her problem. But to his chagrin Sue did not want his "excellent" wisdom. Remember, Sue like most women is concerned with building relationship through sharing information, but there is something else that we men don't understand. Sue processes her day by talking about the details of the relationships and events they experienced. She usually isn't looking for answers but wants Ed to help her explore her feelings about the event, and why she acted in that manner or what is going on behind the scene in the lives of the people around her.

When Sue wants to go into all the details of what is happening in her life it is good for her to have female friends who will listen. Nationally known family expert, James Dobson states that men can't meet all the emotional needs of a woman and so she needs to develop a circle of female friends. Women "get it" when they share the details of an experience with each other. If Sue wants to relate with Ed then she cannot give him all the details of every situation as she would to another woman. She needs to give Ed the CliffsNotes version of what happened. When she sees his eyes glaze over she needs to stop the detail of her story and bring it to a conclusion. She has gone beyond his ability to comprehend or exceeded his interest level or capacity on this topic. Sue can keep Ed engaged longer if she makes him a more active part of her conversation by asking his opinion or soliciting a response rather than making her story a long lecture in which he can't make a point or respond in some way. If Ed seeks to break in with a comment or asks her a question of clarification she will keep him more engaged by interrupting her narrative and interact with him. He wants to know Sue values his input.

The Conversational goal of Men: Problem Solving, Facts

Ed isn't always in tune with Sue about the amount of talking time she needs. There was a cartoon with a man and woman sitting together in front of a television. He looks over to her and says, "We have a few minutes before the game... Quick! How was your day?" Some may chuckle about this and others may have an indignant sigh about his insensitivity to her real need, but to him he was trying to meet her need. He knew that is what women need and want, so he was going to try to do his part. When men don't understand the conversational goals of women, they won't always pursue it correctly.

Ed tends to want to talk about how to solve the problems in life. Listen to him talk about politics, religion, work and sports. He talks about how to fix the problems of our country, or how a leader is handling a certain situation. He wants to understand the details about God and how He works and what He expects out of people. He talks about sports and the thrill of victory and the agony of defeat and how to play a better game. Why is Ed so taken with the logic games, the shoot 'em up video games where he has to defeat the enemy, or even the programming of the computer? He is focused on them because they are all problem-solving situations. Why does he come home and watch the news? To have compassion on those hurting from the latest disaster or to get frustrated by the new laws that congress passed today. He wants to be informed so he can have facts to use in his conversation tomorrow and so he can make correct decisions or have the kind of information he can use in problem solving debates or conversations with others.

There can be frustrations when a relationship-oriented woman talks with a problem-solving man. Ed may not like to go into a lot of detail like Sue does. She, however, wants to talk through the details of the day and he wants to solve her problems when he hears what is going on. Sue wants him to help explore her feelings. Ed takes what he hears, processes it as a problem and comes up with a solution. She is not looking for a solution, but someone to hear her out and affirm her, or commiserate with her. If Sue rejects Ed's problem solving advice he will get frustrated because he doesn't think that what he has to say is valued by her. He then asks himself, "What's the use in saying anything? Sue never listens to anything I have to say!" Sometimes she even gets frustrated with my response, so why try?"If Sue wants to avoid being a frustration to Ed she must, point blank, explain to him that when she is telling him what went on in her day, that she is doing this to vent or process the events of the day and when she wants his help to solve a problem she will ask for it.

If Sue has a problem that she constantly talks about and does not accept any of Ed's solutions for a long time, she needs to stop talking to Ed about her problem and take his advice and work out a solution. Otherwise Ed will grow weary with the conversation because it is going nowhere and that frustrates his logic and problem solving skills. Sue has to realize that they got married for a purpose. Marriage formed a unit in which they were to become stronger together. For that to happen Sue has to understand the needs and perspective of Ed when she communicates with him just as he needs to understand her needs and perspective. It is easy to have the expectation that the other should understand our motives and needs in communication. But the fact of the matter is that many couples minimize or overlook their responsibility to learn to understand the needs each has in communication. Men and women have different needs when it comes to the nature of communication. We must become students of our mates and discover what they need and the kind of conversation that energizes them as well as what frustrates them.

Understanding the Feminine Mystique

When Ed takes Sue out for a special night he is looking for a good time with her. He wants them to share experiences. He enjoys taking Sue into his element, or for her to just be with him while he participates in a sporting event and then go out to celebrate afterwards. Ed wants a companion to enjoy experiencing life together. He likes Sue to support him and be there for him as he is involved in his activities.

Sue's perspective of a romantic evening can be very different than his. Her motivation may not be only to have new experiences, but also to connect with Ed. This is accomplished by catching up on what has been happening in his life or them talking about the interests that are important to both of them. She doesn't want to be distracted by the mundane things of life. Sue wants to feel special and know that he enjoys doing things with her, even if he's not around his friends and hobbies. She wants this time to be a celebration of their love. Sue wants to connect with Ed because being part of his life is a cherished need. When Ed takes her to places she likes without his having to be told, or when he buys Sue gifts that he *knows* she will like, then that is telling her that she has connected with him in relationship. When Ed remembers her birthday or their anniversary it declares to her that she is important and their relationship is a priority in his thinking.

Ed often wonders why Sue is so slow to reveal what she wants from him. She won't tell Ed what she wants because she wants to see if he really knows her. Sue wants to know if he has been paying attention to her needs, likes, concerns and values. When he attends to her needs and is aware of the relationship he has with her, then she knows he is connected with her. This touches her soul. It gives her security in the relationship and it fulfills her.

The above paragraphs should enlighten men as to why your woman doesn't always tell you what they want but she expects you to know it. She wants you to show that you are paying attention to her, valuing her and listening to what she is saying. Remember how attentive you were to her needs while dating? Why would you stop paying attention to her after marriage? She recognizes that when you stop doing special things for her that you actually stopped paying attention to her.

Each time Ed does something for Sue because he *knows* that is what she wants, he shows her that he values her and that she is very important to him. It doesn't always have to be the big things that he does, although there are times that will delight Sue greatly. That is not something Ed could or should do all the time. The small things Ed does for his wife catch her attention and speak volumes to her.

I have found that this is something my wife enjoys. She likes the ninety nine cent ice cream cones from McDonald's. When I am out in the evening I will sometimes stop and get one to take home to surprise her. She also likes breakfast sandwiches at Big Apple Bagel and sometimes on a Sunday morning I'll go out and buy her one and have it there when she wakes up. She likes those little things.

What does your wife like you to do for her? Some women like flowers or candy, or to be taken to a favorite restaurant or maybe she likes a spontaneous outing to the movie theater, or a weekend get-away. You need to do more than know what things she needs; you need to surprise her with them on occasion. That keeps your marriage interesting and is an expression of your love for her, that you have been paying attention to her and you want her to feel special. You did things like that before marriage. Did you stop because you won the prize? She may take it personally when you no longer do any of those special things for her like you used to do. She may reason that she is not as valuable to you now that you have her. She needs you to show her that you are not taking her for granted and that you prize her still.

When Sue feels Ed has connected with her, knows that he values her, and meets her needs, then physical intimacy can be a powerful expression in which she gives herself fully to him. You could say that a woman is a lot like dynamite with a long fuse. The fuse has to be lit through communication and sharing life events, past experiences, thoughts, dreams, concerns and feelings. Sue likes Ed to remember specifics about their life together and as they talk about these things she likes to savor these thoughts for quite a while. The result is that there will be spontaneous reaction that leads to sexual explosion. Usually her sexual expression comes from her emotional needs being met through communication in its many forms. These needs are not met by a two minute conversation. This needs to be a regular part of life as you work them into your daily conversation and contact with her. Sue may need to be wooed by Ed for a day or two before being ready for that special intimate time together.

> A man is not naturally intuitive to a woman's needs.
>
> It is important to pay attention to the needs of your wife.

These facts are very important for men to understand. A man is not naturally intuitive to a woman's needs and will therefore only act on his feelings or urges. It is important to pay attention to the needs of your wife and that you don't live in your own little world all the time. Sports, computer, hobbies and TV make up the world many men live in and the wife does not feel like a significant part of his life. Instead some feel like an outsider who is there to fulfill his needs for food, housekeeping and sex.

18

Love is about entering the world of the other. Think about her, pay attention to her, notice what she likes, listen to what she says and take her seriously. When you allow that information to create an understanding by which you relate to her it is much easier to show her that she is the most important person in the world to you. You cannot convince her of that by your words alone for that truth must also be shown to her.

Chapter Two: Men and Sex

Sue always wondered why she and Ed could be angry with each other or not getting along and then after they had sex Ed would think everything was all right and that the problems had been settled. It just didn't make sense to her! She would still be frustrated that nothing had been talked out, settled or changed, but Ed would be perfectly content. All is well in his world. Nothing had been resolved, nothing had been discussed, and all he'd done was to have sex! There was no significant communication during or after sex. No exchange of information. Yet Ed would feel absolutely fulfilled and at peace in their relationship. Why are there two different results in their minds? Does Ed have no soul? Is he so shallow that he only values and needs physical relationship? It does not compute in the mind of many women.

Sue has such a hard time relating to what motivates Ed in the area of sex. He wants to touch her (intimately) and sometimes for no reason at all. Sue wonders if she is just a sexual object to fulfill his physical needs; and, by the way, what needs are really being met? Is Ed just an animal in his desires, doing it for the sake of doing it? Sue sees nothing being accomplished with those touches or those "quickies". Often sex for her is a response to satisfy him because she loves him, but it does not have the meaning to her that it does for him. It is often just one more annoyance in her life or an opportunity to please him. After all, Sue knows that everything gets accomplished through good communication and so if Ed would just try a little harder they could be so much closer. Sue just doesn't "get it" from her man's perspective. He is so different from her in what she needs. Will they ever get anywhere if he doesn't learn to communicate? Sue needs to realize that men are wired differently than women in terms of what gives meaning to their life, even when they are able to communicate well.

> *Sue needs to realize that men are wired differently than women in terms of what gives meaning to their life, even when they are able to communicate well.*

Feldhahn is an excellent research writer. In her book "For Women Only"[3] one chapter addresses the need of sex for the man. She comes to her conclusions through interviews and questionnaires. Her points in one chapter describe the significance of sex to a man in very telling ways.

1. **Fulfilling sex makes him feel loved and desired.** She goes on to say that many men seem to live in a deep sense of loneliness that is quite foreign to us oh-so-relational women.

2. **Fulfilling Sex gives him confidence**. One person she interviewed said "What happens in the bedroom really does affect how I see the next day at the office." Another wrote: "Sex is a release of day-to-day pressures…seems to make everything else better."

3. **If she doesn't want to, I feel incredible rejection**." One man says: "She doesn't understand that I feel loved by sexual caressing, and if she doesn't want to, I feel incredible rejection." Another says "When she says no, I feel that I am REJECTED. 'No' is not to sex – as she might feel. It is no to me as I am. And I am vulnerable as I ask or initiate. It's plain and simple rejection."

4. **Your lack of desire can send him into depression**. If your sexual desire gives your husband a sense of well-being and confidence, you can understand why an ongoing perception that you don't desire him would translate into a nagging lack of confidence, withdrawal and depression.

As you contemplate what Shaunti just said recognize that sex has a profound meaning in the depth of a man's being. It gives him confidence in the relationship; withholding sex can cause a deep feeling of personal rejection. From his perspective it gives him the sense of being loved by you. Whereas the woman thinks of communication as being the strong bonding agent for relationship, the man sees sex as the bonding agent that gives a relationship meaning. Just as your loneliness is quieted by meaningful communication, his intense loneliness is quieted by meaningful sex. We go down the wrong path when we think the other's needs are met in the same way that ours are met.

How much of what was just said about the importance of sex to your husband did you realize before you read the above section? How will that, or should that affect the way you respond to him?

Even though the wife deeply loves her husband and is willing to meet his sexual needs, most women don't understand what sex accomplishes for a man and his well-being. Because most men don't fully understand why they need sex so much and so regularly doesn't negate its importance in his life. He just knows that he needs it. That is why this teaching is so important and must be understood. If a woman wants that deep intimacy with him, then she needs to realize that she must communicate in two languages; male and female. To not understand "male" leads to hurts and frustration for him and it doesn't allow the relationship to grow and experience the depth of intimacy that it could.

The Path to Understanding

Sue feels connected and emotionally fulfilled when there is communication and sharing of thoughts, events, concerns, fears, joys and dreams with Ed. That touches the heart of her being. When Sue is fulfilled she feels connected to Ed. Some men can connect very easily with their wives but for Ed it is something that he is going to have to learn. There are many times when Ed appreciates those good talks and really enjoys the deep conversations with Sue. In these times he feels connected to her. No matter how much he enjoys this meaningful communication it just does not touch his soul and bring him the same level of fulfillment that it does to Sue. On the other hand, sex does not consistently touch the soul of Sue like it does for Ed. Sex accomplishes that same kind of fulfillment for Ed as communication and emotional connection does for Sue. Both are different and that is not wrong. God put variety in us to learn to patiently learn about the other.

- What communication accomplishes for a woman, sex does for a man.
- To the depth that communication fulfills a woman's soul sex fulfills a man's soul.
- The way communications attracts the soul of a woman, sex attracts the soul of a man.
- The way in which a man and a woman are fulfilled are different and must be respected and valued.
- Sex often opens men to communication and meaningful communication often opens women to sex.

Did I say it in enough different ways that you both "get it"? This does not mean that men don't enjoy communication and that women don't enjoy sex. It's just saying that they accomplish different purposes for each in the way they fulfill the soul. The creator has hard-wired each differently. When you accept the difference of the other and appreciate it without thinking you have to change the other to become like you, then you have the foundation for making your relationship stronger.

So, when your husband touches you (or, you might call it groping), when he has sex, whether it seems like it couldn't really have been a meaningful experience, the fact remains, sex touches his soul. It makes him feel connected to you. It accomplishes the same kind of connection you feel when you have really meaningful communication and emotional exchange. The result of feeling connected may or may not bring on an openness of sharing, but it does make him feel connected to you as well as fulfilled. No, that does not mean you will fully understand it, but you do need to know it and accept it.

One day Sue and Ed got into kind of a heated discussion because he was always grabbing her when she walked by or when they sat together. He smiled and said, if you feel like that when I touch you, then you will understand how I feel when you go into minute detail about the day's events. It seems like what you are telling me is more detail than I want or can follow and it doesn't make sense, but you seem to feel better when you are done. That day the light went on for both of them about understanding the needs of the other, and the importance of learning to enjoy this part of the opposite sex and appreciate what it means to them. Think about the term "opposite sex". You are different physically, emotionally, and in your sexual needs.

Men don't fully understand how sex impacts their life and usually don't know how to explain it to their wives; they just know that their drive is strong and unrelenting. Dr. Juli Slattery in her book "NO MORE HEADACHES, Enjoying Sex & Intimacy in Marriage"[4] talks about important aspects of how sex impacts the whole being of a man. When you understand how dynamically sex impacts him in the following ways it will help you gain a better insight into his inner being and put into proper perspective the heart of your man.

It is in chapter six of Dr. Slattery's book that she goes into this detail to help women understand their husband's sexuality and why sex is so important to their marriage. This teaching allows you to be more appreciative of his deep seated need of sex. She explains how sex is important to a man physically, emotionally, spiritually and relationally. I have paraphrased some of her findings under each point.

-Sex is a Physical Need. Men have a legitimate physical necessity to have sex. None of us has to make an excuse because we are hungry or thirsty or even tired. These are legitimate needs that we have on a regular basis. The need your husband has for sexual release is just as real as our need for food, water and rest. Men have a biological drive, because of their levels of testosterone to have sex.

There is a difference between men and women in their drive to have sex. Women are more connected to and driven by their emotions when it comes to sex. Men, on the other hand, can be aroused without any emotional attachment. He can wake up in the morning without any forethought of sex in any way and be ready.

-Sex is an Emotional Need. Most men recognize how important sexual fulfillment is to their confidence and masculinity. A man can take on great challenges when this area of his life is fulfilled.

She quotes Dr. Archibald Hart who has done extensive research on male sexuality. He says that men equate their maleness to their sexuality. When men approach their wives for sex and are refused, then they actually personalize that refusal of not wanting sex as a rejection of them as a person. Dr. Hart quotes Feldhahn from the same quote given above when a woman says "no" (See # 3 of Feldhahn's quote at beginning of chapter.) Men are very sensitive to their wife's refusal. He feels personal rejection. However when the emotional part of sex is welcomed it draws him into deeper intimacy.

Dr. Hart goes on to make a very telling statement to women. "You cannot love him as a husband but reject him sexually." He continues in his statement making it very clear that you cannot separate his sexuality from who is in relationship to you. A woman can compartmentalize her sexuality, but a man can't do that.

24

-Sex is a Spiritual Need. A man has a hard time relating his unrelenting need for sex with the spiritual part of his life. He struggles with his sexual temptations. He is very visual and when he looks at women his thoughts can turn very sexual in an instant. Men involved with porn struggle with guilt and therefore it is hard to approach God with confidence when they pray, or seek to worship wholeheartedly. In such times it is hard to feel he has full acceptance by God. Such guilt can even cause him to doubt his salvation when he is acting out his sexual desires. Often men find it hard to talk with anyone, especially their wives about this need. Legitimate expressions of their sexual need are very important to his spiritual well being.

-Sex is a Relational Need. Sexual fulfillment and expression are very important elements of maintaining and enjoying the marriage relationship. Sex allows your husband to relate to you in a more affectionate manner. He is able to be more considerate and thoughtful after sex. Have you noticed that difference in your man after sex? You may wonder how that act of sex could have meant all that much to him, yet that act made a world of difference in the way he related to you. Is that really so? That is not your imagination. That is the reality of what sex does for him in his ability to relate to you. His orgasm literally helps him feel emotionally closer to you. That effect is explained in more detail in the section that talks about oxytocin.

You want your husband to be understanding of you and your need. Hopefully this section has given you a perspective of your husband that helps you to be more understanding of him as well.

The teaching of evolution has an impact on how some women view this "primitive" need in man. They tend to think they can reform their man, or help him evolve into a person who is more relational like they are. Some have even wrongfully thought that women have evolved more than men. The fact is, the creator made both different, and so we don't have to change or correct one to become like the other. We are to learn to embrace the differences and appreciate them and do what we can to help the other feel complete and fulfilled. That is why it is called a relationship, for you both need to work together for the other's benefit. Why would you need someone else if you both saw and understood life in the same way? Differences in people make us stop and realize that our view is not the only one, and our way is not the only right way. When we learn from people who have another perspective we broaden our awareness as well as enjoyment of life.

Her Communication

When Sue starts talking with Ed and he cuts her off and makes her think that what she has to share is unimportant, what does that do to her? It makes her feel upset or angry. It probably makes her feel like she is unimportant or that her needs are insignificant to Ed. He has cut off that which is so valuable in developing and maintaining relationship. She is hurt! How does she respond? Will she say: "If he doesn't value me then why should I value him?" The problem is that neither Ed nor Sue usually understands how they reject each other, or how much they hurt the other by their unperceived dismissal of the other's needs. When they see each other's reaction they may ask, "What's the big deal in what I did or said? What did I do wrong that they should be so offended? I meant no harm. They should just understand me."

It is imperative to the relationship that Ed understands the importance of communication to Sue and what it accomplishes for her. Sometimes it is not enough for Sue to just talk, but she needs to teach Ed why it is important that he listens when she has a need. Sue's girlfriends understand the need to explore the details of what goes on in her life, but Ed doesn't have a clue about how to achieve that for Sue. Her girlfriends want to hear every detail, but Ed's eyes glaze over about 10-15 minutes into Sue's details of the event. But that doesn't mean that Ed can't learn how to be there for Sue. She might look for ways to learn how to communicate with him with fewer words and less detail and description and by letting him be more involved in the conversation. Ed will find it easier to follow if he engages Sue throughout the conversation by asking questions for clarification.

Sue would do well to help Ed understand what such conversation does for her. She should choose the right times to teach him about how he needs to be there for her concerns. She would be wise to avoid talking to him about how he can be there for her when they are in a "heated" discussion. The more he learns about Sue's needs in the matter of communication the better he can respond to her and engage those needs.

Ed and Sue came up with some guidelines to help meet the need she had for communication. They established a regular time to talk each day. They set aside twenty minutes each day to share the daily events and how they felt about them. It became their time to talk about urgent issues and daily happenings. It was something Sue could count on each day to connect with Ed. Sue agreed not to dump on Ed as soon as he entered the house after work. She gave him time to catch his thoughts and relax a bit. She didn't give him blow by blow detail of everything each time she told him about her day. Sue didn't overwhelm him with every single detail of each event. She focused on more bullet point details with short explanations. Your guidelines may be different, but it is important to set up a regular time of communication and guidelines that will facilitate this communication time.

As Ed came to appreciate and engage this time with Sue she began to add more detail to her explanations. Ed needed to know how Sue's mind worked. He found out that Sue's thoughts kept bouncing around in her mind and made her feel unsettled until she expressed them. That is why she had to get them out and tell him all about them. Sue felt more confident and at peace after she talked out the events of the day and what was on her mind. That meant that she needed to understand why she had to share these thoughts. When she understood what drove her she was then able to properly help Edward better understand what was going on in her mind and what motivated her. She didn't expect that Ed would "get it". Could he ever understand why she needed to talk about all the details of her day? When she explained her motivation in a clear way and why it was so important to her, the light started to brighten in Ed's understanding. Men respond much better when you explain your reasoning and purpose. Men are black and white and need it explained. Most are not intuitive in communication.

A woman's mind is kind of like a pinball machine where the ball keeps getting knocked from one pin to another, and sometimes at very fast speeds. During a game the ball goes out of play when it slips by the flippers into the hole in the bottom. Your wife's mind is like a ball that keeps getting banged around from one side to the other and the only outlet is for her to talk about what is going on in her mind. Then her mind experiences contentment and peace.

Sue needed to think through how she was going to explain how her mind works so Ed could understand it. She came to the conclusion that it

27

could be something as simple as "Ed, I need some communication-time with you so I can settle my thoughts because they are running rampant in my mind right now." She already knew that if she said; "We need to talk" or "Let's talk" Ed would want to know what he did wrong. Or he wants to know specifics and say; "What do you want to talk about Sue?" Ed just doesn't "get it" that Sue just needs to talk about what has been happening in their lives. Most of the time Sue doesn't have an agenda, she just wants an *information passing session* with Ed; just a "touching base" kind of meeting with her man. She decided the best way to approach Ed would be to express her need with a simple request like, "I just need to touch base with you about what is going on. Can we take some time now?" This helped him identify the kind of conversation she needed with him. She found that he actually enjoyed engaging that because he knew what she wanted or needed.

Sue learned an important lesson when she took the time to inform Ed about the importance of touching base with her. He now knew what exactly she needed. Most women think it is stupid that a man doesn't know how to just talk and share thoughts and feelings without there being a topic. When Sue realized that Ed didn't "get it" and it seemed like there was a shade pulled down over their potential conversation she then took the initiative to teach him what she needed in their conversations. She learned how to be specific, for her man's need for black and white communication that doesn't beat around the bush. She looked for ways to make her kind of conversation a part of their time together. It helped when they decided that something as simple as dinner-talk with no TV or a little conversation at bed time filled their need. Sue found out that Ed opened up more in conversation when going for a walk together or if she would go to the hardware store with him. He likes Sue to do things with him instead of just sitting around talking at home. Sue discovered that her tone of voice was so important when she discussed her needs in communication. She wanted to show her respect for him in the way she addressed him.

When you understand your own needs and are able to express them to your partner, then you are ready to understand why his style of communication is so important to him.

His Communication

When Ed approaches Sue sexually and she cuts him off or pushes him away, he experiences the very same kind of feelings of rejection Sue feels when he doesn't want to listen or take her conversation seriously. She doesn't think her refusal should affect Ed because she is not interested at that time and he should just wait for a better time, for instance, when she is ready. She thinks that because sex does not have such a high priority to her that it shouldn't be all that important to him. What Sue fails to see is that he is, at that point, feeling the very same kind of rejection that she has when he won't listen or engage her in conversation. He feels sharply rejected when she pushes him away or puts him off and doesn't treat his need for sex as something important or significant. Such a refusal can make Ed feel like he is unimportant to her. Ed's need for sex is tied to his need to feel connected to Sue. This is the connection that makes him feel a part of her and assuages his loneliness.

Just as Sue is frustrated when Ed fails to freely engage in communication, so he also gets frustrated when she refuses to freely engage in sex with him on a regular basis. Suppose that Ed refused to engage in any kind of conversation with Sue for a week? Would that set well with her? Yet she thinks that it should not bother Ed when his need for sex is being minimized and refused for long periods. Dennis Rainey, nationally known family speaker and writer comments on the importance of this truth as he talks about a man's feeling of rejection when she doesn't take his needs seriously:

> *"When a man is rejected often enough, he typically internalizes his anger, his hurt, and his disappointment until such time when the rejection drives him to one of several reactions—none of them are good. Either he will give up on the relationship or he will seek alternative sexual outlets such as pornography, or he might compromise his wedding vows by pursuing female affirmation elsewhere."[5]*

Just because Sue might not have that need or drive in her life doesn't mean that Ed's needs can be written off without hurt or consequences. If Sue doesn't take his sexual needs seriously then she needs to ask herself why Ed's needs are not a priority for her or why isn't he that important to her? His need for sex is just as real as her need for communication. Why is she willing to hurt Ed that way and think it shouldn't bother him? Such thinking is based in the thought that it is easier to write off a person's needs when we minimize their importance and therefore don't take them seriously. We base our reasoning on what we perceive for the other person rather than what their true need is.

Shortly after that point was made in Sue's thinking it was driven home again when she found herself listening to a radio broadcast by Dannah Gresh who was talking about women and sexuality. She heard Dannah say that "we live in such a society where sex is used to get what we want instead of using it to meet the needs of the other." She said "we need to stop offering the excuse of being tired or having a headache and take our husband's needs seriously." Dannah concluded her comments by making this insightful observation about a woman's response to her man; "If we start giving him what he needs he will then give you what you need." Hearing an expert confirm her conclusion helped Sue to have confidence in the conclusion she reached about meeting Ed's needs.

After I wrote this portion of the book I found a letter about a man's relationship in an advice column in our local newspaper that expressed the very thoughts that Mr. Rainey discussed above. The writer's thoughts are insightful into the problem right down to his suggestions about how he would resolve the issue. Notice that even though he says everything else is good in his marriage he is actually considering divorce as part of his solution to get out of a situation where she does not value him and his need for sex. This man is really desperate and his wife doesn't seem to have a clue as to its serious consequences to their marriage and how it is killing her husband. He is actively seeking to resolve the situation but she refuses to even discuss it. The article was titled: **30-year-old wife goes months without interest in sex.**[6]

"Dear Annie: My wife and I are both 30 and have been married for five years. We have a toddler. The problem is, over the past few years, my wife has cut down sex to roughly once every couple of months. I do what I can to keep her happy and have even bargained with her to get sex by offering to take her out to eat at her favorite restaurant or giving back massages, but she won't discuss it. As soon as I bring it up, she gets angry and it puts her in a bad mood. My wife doesn't seem to care about my needs at all, and I can't help but resent her for doing this to me. The rest of our marriage is solid, but this one issue has me considering divorce. I don't

want to cheat on her, but I want to be with someone who cares about me. I can deal with sex as infrequently as once a month, but there are stretches where it's been half a year... Is there a different way to having this conversation so she can see my point of view?"

What would you say to that woman? How would you encourage that man? Do you hear his heart and the importance of his need of sex? If you go for long periods of time without engaging in sex, do you think that such a rejection of your husband also drives him to frustration and bewilderment? How do you think you ought to respond to him? How often do you think you should respond to him? What would he say if you initiated having sex more often? What would he say if you asked him if he was getting enough sex from you to satisfy him? Ladies, does this man's frustration sound like yours when your man doesn't engage you in meaningful conversation?

Are you seeing more fully the importance of both communication and sex in your relationship? When she lacks the experience of having fulfilling regular communication and he lacks having meaningful regular sex then each is being denied one of the most important needs of their lives. Do you both know how to "communicate" with each other in a manner that leaves them satisfied? Does the way you "communicate" show that they are the most important person on earth to you?

The Importance of a Kiss

Another method of communication is without words. As much as the sexual need offers the physical contact that brings great fulfillment, don't neglect other forms of physical contact, like the hug and kiss.

Gilbert Morris' historical series THE HOUSE OF WINSLOW is a sequence of stories about a man who comes to America on the Mayflower. His family is followed through American history as a means of introducing the reader to the major players who forged the direction of our country as well as to the significant events that made history. I read about twenty six volumes in the series. In each book the main character ends up getting married. The relationship is developed as Morris talks about the woman's eyes and then the first kiss. There was something about that kiss that lingered in their mind and drew them together. As the main character of each book thought about that first kiss it became the focal point of their relationship that culminated in marriage. The kiss was a common thread through this historical series. If you think about it, a kiss is also a common element in the romance people have experienced through the ages and more than likely in your romance story as well. Do you remember your first kiss?

Kissing is important. It was significant in courtship and it should also be essential in marriage. It draws people together and stimulates great passion. It is our way of connecting with someone special. A kiss is for someone very special, for someone you love, for someone you are inviting into your space. One writer described kissing as a physical symbol of a couples affection and love. It is a way, without words, to show the other person that you have a deep connection with them and a love for them. It may just be a peck on the lips or cheeks, but that little peck is important. Then there are those times that you give that special person a long passionate kiss. I remember times during my marriage when my wife came up and planted a long passionate kiss on me, wow! It would revitalize and energize me. It did something to our relationship right then that I always appreciated.

The chemistry of sex and kissing will be discussed in later chapter but let me introduce interesting facts you won't want to kiss good-bye. Serotonin levels spike while kissing, these create obsessive thoughts about your partner. Also levels of oxytocin increase while kissing. Oxytocin is known as the love hormone which induces a feeling of bonding and attachment.

Do you value the opportunity to give your husband or wife a long passionate kisses? Such kisses are important for they express a special connectedness. This fact has motivated me in my pre-marital counseling, over the years, to encourage couples to make kissing a regular and important part of their marriage. Often I told the couple that as much as they enjoy a passionate kiss now, they need to continue such kissing through their marriage. I challenged them to give a passionate kiss at least once a week that lasts for at least ten seconds. That doesn't sound like a lot of time, but it can keep romance alive, and the relationship interesting for the couple. How much do you value kissing?

Several websites even talked about various health benefits related to kissing. You may find some results surprising. These findings may also give you another reason to kiss more frequently.

Kissing can make your heart rate go up to 110 beats per minute. You exercise more than 30 facial muscles in a kiss. Saliva exchange boosts your immune system. A 5-minute kiss can burn 12 calories, so make your kisses longer and do it more often! Relieves stress! Kissing for long periods of time naturally reduces hormonal stress. Kissing can give your self-esteem a positive jolt! Kissing makes you feel appreciated and helps improve your state of mind. Aside from stabilizing cardiovascular activity, kissing can also decrease blood pressure and cholesterol. Endorphins produced by kissing are 200 times more powerful than morphine. This is a safer way to get high.

Kissing is more than a physical act. It is something that touches our soul. Kissing increases our awareness of our emotional connection. In the benefits listed above for kissing, why do you think it would decrease blood pressure? Kissing reminds you that you are loved by your spouse and that helps take away some of those stresses of life. It produces endorphins that generate pleasure. In our hard times of life don't we need more of those good feelings? Go ahead and read the quote above again and this time take better note of the benefits of kissing. You might want to do a Google search for "benefits of kissing". It will provide some additional interesting information.

Some women don't want to kiss often because they fear that passionate kissing will lead to him wanting sex. Kissing is important. It reminds you that you are in a relationship rather than a contract with the other. It is a thoughtful expression of our desire for or love of our spouse. Kissing is one of the intimacies reserved for that special closeness between couples. It tells the other that you care about them and that they are important to you. Sometimes you kiss to let them know that they are really special to you. Even though kissing can lead to a romantic time, it can also just be your way of saying that you are glad that you are married to them. A passionate kiss is a nice way to welcome your spouse home and can be your unspoken message for them to think about and anticipate tonight!

Many women avoid passionate kissing because of the "threat" of sex more often that they want. Let me say something that can help defuse your fear. Talk to him openly and forthright about your concerns. Tell him that you want to give him a passionate kiss more frequently. Sometimes it may lead to sex, but most of the time it won't. Tell him that he is important to you and you want to show him by giving him these special kisses. Then tell him that these kisses are a reminder of how much you love him. You want him to understand that you want him to appreciate and enjoy you right then. Make life interesting for him and let him know how much he means to you. There is a flip side to this. When he knows how much you care about him in this way, most will tend to be more loving to you. It's really a win-win situation.

Men, this previous paragraph is important. We think that kissing ought to lead to more. We think that such kissing ought to always have the perk of sexual touch. Don't be so quick to go there in your response every time. Enjoy your wife and what she is doing with a passionate kiss. Hold her close and enjoy her presence. Just enjoy and the kiss. Don't suggest anything else, no matter how hard it is to restrain your actions in that moment. You may find that such a response may or may not yield the results you desire later that evening, but allow her to control that moment. Such a response does satisfy your wife and that should be your priority. Your wife needs to know that you care for her. She wants you to be "taken" with her for that moment. She wants you to anticipate her. This is her way of telling you that she doesn't always want all the physical contact that leads to sex that you do. She needs to be able to kiss you, hug you and be held by you without it always ending in sex.

If kissing has not been a prominent part of your relationship why not consider making it so. One counselor said that when a couple comes to her with problems, one of the first questions she asks them is how often they kiss. It tells her something about what is missing in their relationship.

Determine to kiss more frequently. All kisses don't have to be passionate. Establish your kissing routines. By all means, kiss in front of the kids. It shows them that you are in love. My dad used to come home from work and plant a big kiss on mom in front of us kids. We knew that he love her. He would laugh and enjoy her in such a neat way. Kiss when you leave each other in the morning for it makes the beginning of your day positive. When you get home a welcome kiss says that you are glad to see them and you are glad that you are both together. Then don't forget a nice kiss to close your day before you go to bed. Also you may want to look for opportunities to ambush the other with a surprise kiss on occasion. Guys, you will score points with her if it is only a kiss that has no other implications, if you get the drift. Those kissing contacts, which may seem relatively insignificant, are really important and you will come to enjoy them. Regular kisses mean that you are not just a roommate, or a fellow employee, but two people in a significant, committed relationship. You can always make time for a kiss. A kiss doesn't disrupt your schedule enough to put you behind, but it can give a pleasant jolt to your attitude as you leave home.

Suppose that you don't like to kiss much, is it still important for you to kiss? Kissing your spouse may be very important to them and you are denying them something they need because you have little interest in it. Perhaps you need to ask yourself why you don't like to kiss. Is it because you never saw it at home? Why does it make you feel uncomfortable? You might find kissing more pleasurable if you do it more regularly. Before you kiss your loved one every day for the next week or so, take some time before hand to think about why you love them and what you appreciate about them. Then allow your emotion to express your appreciation and love to them without words but by your kiss. Again, I'm not talking about a peck on the cheek that you give to your aunt Jeanette, but a nice wet kiss with some passion. Enjoy the love of your life!

Along with your kiss, be sure to include hugs as a part of your routine. I have come to realize the power of a hug. I was a pastor for 39 years and we were a hugging church. The widows had not had physical contact with people and when they were hugged you could see them brighten up. I've been at many funerals and people who are hurting run to each other and they hug and cry. There is something about that hug that gives the hurting person strength to face a very difficult loss and realize they are not alone. There are those times in our life when we haven't seen a parent, child or friend for some time and when we see them we can't help but hug them. That hug helps us to reconnect.

Make hugs a regular routine in your home. When the other comes home from a hard day give them a hug and just hold them for a while. Allow them to feel secure in your arms and remind them how much you love them with your tender embrace. When you come home and are full of energy give the other a wild, fun loving hug. Laugh together and just enjoy each other's presence. These are things you enjoyed in your courtship. Why have such common tender moments become so insignificant and uncommon to so many couples that they no longer employ them in their relationship? Why have we down-graded our ranking in the relationship that we don't think that our needs are unimportant? Marriage is about relationship and the busyness of life sometimes clouds the fact that we love our mate and that they are the most important person on earth to us.

I close this section with a few quotes on hugs and kissing. These are just reminders that hugs and kisses can have a profound effect on our whole being. They should be taken seriously as well as practice regularly with our spouse.

Hugs and Kisses

-*Release my body with your lips, and stir my soul with the heat of your kiss. -- Anonymous*

-*A hug is a handshake from the heart. ~Author Unknown*

-*A kiss is the true love expression of the soul. – Anonymous*

-*Your hugs and kisses are like the stars that light up my life when things get dark. ~Author Unknown*

-*When you kiss me without uttering a single word you speak to my soul – Unknown*

-*Sometimes it's better to put love into hugs than to put it into words. ~Unknown*

-*When [he] kisses you he isn't doing anything else. You're his whole universe and the moment is eternal because he doesn't have any plans and isn't going anywhere. Just kissing you...it's overwhelming. – Anon*

-*A kiss without a hug is like a flower without the fragrance. ~Proverb*

Helping Her to Become More Willing

Men, as you read this chapter about your need of sex, your thoughts resound with a loud affirmation! "These are the words that express my needs. Now my wife just needs to read this and I hope that will finally help her to understand why I have this great need of sex. Perhaps she will understand why she needs to be there for me and I won't be so frustrated and feel rejected so much."

However, even though one understands a truth, that doesn't change a person's actions or responses to us. Marriage is more than expectations and actions; it is a relationship in which these actions take place out of love and concern for the other. Just because you have a great need of sex doesn't mean that you have a right to demand sex or think that every request will be fulfilled just because you ask for it. Relationship means that you are aware of her as a person. It means that you seek to understand some of her frustrations and needs that face her each day. She may have been mentally distraught because of kids or because of people at work. She can't just turn the events of the day off and instantly have passion for you. She needs relationship with you before she can give herself to you.

Perhaps that is why you need to listen to her when you get home. This is a time to be empathetic and let her unwind or unload on you. Pay attention to what she says. Ask questions for clarification and let her express her feelings. Perhaps you could ask, "What can I do to help you through this?" "How can I help you?" "Do you just need a listening ear or are you looking for a solution?" What does your wife need from you?

You can capture your wife's attention by showing emotion and passion to her without always making it about sex. Hold your wife, give her a kiss and don't always feel you have to touch her sexually. Kiss her passionately sometimes and let her know how much you love her without making it about sex. Come up behind her and pause to rub her back for a moment and just continue with what you were doing. Such actions will mean more to her than you can imagine.

Understand your wife. Whereas you can be turned on in a second by a touch, or a look or a though, she needs time to get ready for sex. You are easily aroused to have sex and for you that does deepen the relationship. A woman needs relationship with her man before she has meaningful sex.

What can you do in the hours before bed time that prepares your wife for a good evening of love making? What prepares her mind, soul and spirit to give to you physically? If you don't know, have you thought of asking her? Chances are she has told you what she needs at different times, but you just didn't take her seriously. You had one thing on your mind and it blocked out your hearing.

There is a popular advertisement about a certain bunny that keeps on going. They promote the long lasting ability of their alkaline battery. Men are much like this bunny and they also want their wives to always be ready to engage. However, your wife is more like the battery in your cell phone. I have a phone and it needs to be recharged every evening. Sometimes before I go someplace I will put my phone on the charger to bring it up to a fuller charge so it will last the rest of the day. I just want to make sure it has enough power for anything that may arise.

Your wife is like the rechargeable battery and the recharger is you. The events of the day drain her battery and she needs to be recharged by you. How do you go into recharging mode? Whereas you may feel drained by listening to all the details of her day, she is energized by talking about them to you, because you are the one who should care about her and what has been going on in her day. When you see things that need to be done around the house and do them on your own she is energized. When you follow through on her requests to have something done she is energized. When you give her a thoughtful compliment and express what she means to you that energizes her. When you surprise her with flowers, some candy, or take her out to dinner or a weekend away unexpectedly she is energized because then she knows she is special to you. When you give her time to herself on a regular basis by taking care of the kids she is energized. As a student of your wife discover what energizes her.

One of the things couples fail to do after marriage is to continue to date. Many couples have learned the lasting benefits of committing to having a regular date night at least once or twice a month. If all of your dates involve sports, make sure that is what she actually wants to do, or is she going to the sporting event to just be with you. Make sure her needs are also the focus of your date nights as well. Plan a year of dates with the idea of focusing on special interests you both have. Dates with other couples are nice but make sure you plan dates for just the two of you. Some dates allow for conversation and some don't. When on a date make sure there is time to talk about fun things and issues of interest to you both. Don't make it a time to settle your problems and don't focus on work or always talk about the kids. Make the time just about the two of you. Having a regular uninterrupted time to just talk and allow each other to express their concerns and needs is a vital part to strengthen the relationship. Make sure you plan some week-end get a-ways on a regular basis. These are the kinds of things that keep romance alive and energize your wife and give her the freedom to give herself more freely to you.

How can you energize your wife? I've given you some ideas. Now it is up to you to continue to add to that list. What is it that your wife needs and wants from you? How can you be there for her? The key to understanding her needs is to listen to her and take what she says seriously. When you don't understand what she needs then ask her what you can do. That's called communication. It is easy to overlook the obvious. Learn to ask obvious questions to make sure you understand her. It is the wise man that becomes the student of his wife and learns what energizes her and then starts doing it. Relationship means that you attend to each other's needs and that means you are not always on the demanding end.

Chapter Three: Our Passion to Experience Fulfillment

Many women don't fully know why they need to communicate with their husbands just as most men don't fully understand why sex is so important to them. Usually both know what is important but don't always fully understand the "why" of their need.

Communication and sex gives us soul connection and fulfillment in the relationship with the person we love dearly. If you take nothing else away from this book please understand this truth and take it seriously in your relationship...

> *"It's just as important for the man to value the wife's need for communication and emotional fulfillment as it is for the wife to value the man's sexual need in the relationship."*

So, if Ed wants to have a relationship in which Sue is more willing to meet his needs then Sue needs to hear him tell about his day, and she needs him to listen and be concerned about what is happening in her life. This is called two sided conversation. Such conversation may not be easy for Ed because it is not always natural for men to communicate like women, but it is, none the less, something he needs to develop and practice. Some men may talk a lot about their achievements, but don't know how to share what they are feeling during these times. They haven't learned how to reveal what their wives want or need to hear. Ed needs to become a student of his wife so he understands her and her needs. He can do that by asking questions about what makes her tick and when she tells him her concerns he needs to take what she says seriously. When Ed doesn't take Sue seriously it diminishes the importance of their relationship. It tends to treat her as a child rather than a peer.

It took me many years to learn the art of communication in knowing what to talk about with my wife and what she needed to hear from me. Over the years I have come to appreciation the verbal connection between us so much that when we haven't connected for a while I miss it. For many men this has to be learned and it can be a long process. As I have said before, the wife needs to patiently teach her husband what she is looking for in communication, and she needs to tell him why it is so important.

Sue found out that she experienced the same satisfaction in her soul from good communication as Ed does from good sex. Responding to Ed with sex has not always been easy for Sue because she didn't have the same strong sex drive that he does. His appetite for sex was like her appetite for communication. Sue was content with infrequent sex just as he was content with infrequent verbal connection. Sue needed to understand Ed's needs and to value the importance of responding to his sexual advances. In the same way Ed needed to learn how to engage Sue in communication and "talk in her language". When needs are known and understood in the other it is easier to "talk their language" in a way that will fulfill their needs.

Good conversation cannot be demanded but it must be entered into willingly and with interest. Just as a person who wants to learn something and will work to perfect their knowledge in a certain area, so that kind of desire needs to motivate you to connect with your wife in the area of communication. The same is also true concerning sex. Just because Ed has the need for sex doesn't mean that he just demands it and Sue should always be instantly ready. He must be considerate of her feelings and mental health at that time of day or month as well. Sue usually cannot respond instantly and the daily pressures of her life take her mind a thousand miles from any thought of sex. Just because Ed has an urge does not mean that Sue must fulfill that need immediately. His urge does not mean that he does not have to take time to woo his wife, talk with her and take time to meet her needs. Sudden passion is great sometimes, but that's not how it usually goes down nor is such a response a frequent reality in long term relationships. It sells movies but movies aren't always interested in reality. That doesn't mean there won't be passion, it just will not be an every night occurrence. Make sure you make the effort to put passion into your relationship, at a minimum of once a month. Ask your partner how often they realistic need such passion, and what they need from you. Take what they say seriously.

Because of the busyness of life sometimes a couple needs to plan regular times together for sex in order to make sure that sex is a regular routine in their relationship. Ed needs to allow Sue to say no because she is not ready, but she also needs to realize that Ed's need is very important to him if she wants him to feel close to her. When Sue decided to make sure Ed could count on sex regularly she found that even though she wasn't always ready, she did come to enjoy it more frequently, just because she took the opportunity to engage her man in something that is so important to him.

Even though Ed is ready for sex quickly, he needs to woo Sue throughout the day for her to anticipate time with him. To woo a woman has become a lost art for many after marriage as well as for couples who cohabitate. Wooing your wife keeps the spark in your relationship. How do you woo a woman? Ed read one article and the bullet points of what was said included simple things he could do for Sue. The list included such things as: *"Be a gentleman. Be thoughtful and expressive of your feelings. Never forget important dates like her birthday. Listen when she speaks. Do little things for her like personal notes and thinking of you cards"*.[7]

Now that Ed knew that wooing was important to Sue it meant he was committed to looking for ways to make Sue feel special and show her that she is important to him. He thought of some of those neat things he used to do for her before they were married to make her feel special. Ed is smart enough to know that he needs to think from Sue's perspective if he's going to understand what she needs or wants him to do for her. As he thought of ideas he decided that as the occasion presented itself he would do some of those thoughtful things. Then it dawned on Ed that he certainly knew Sue a lot better now than he did before they got married, and knows a lot more of the things she likes. He was going to take that wooing thing more seriously now if that would help bring them closer together in their relationship. He said I'd be a fool if I hadn't learned more about Sue in the last three years. I've got enough sense to pay attention to what my wife enjoys so I can do something about it.

Sue always enjoys being surprised by those unexpected handwritten notes that Ed leaves for her when she finds them later at home or when she gets to work. Ed makes it a practice to text her when he thinks of her throughout the day to let Sue know what is going on in his life. The important thing is that he lets her know that he is thinking about her and that she is important to him. Ed Is learning the importance of communication and he talks with Sue about things they anticipate doing together such as a date night or coming vacation, or the weekend get-a-way they have been planning. Ed sat back at his desk one day after he got a text response from Sue about their date that evening. He said, with a smile on his face and satisfaction in his voice, "I think I'm getting a hang of how to woo my wife."

How Conversation helps Her to Handle Her Day

When Sue has a stressful day or something exciting happens she wants to unload or share with Ed right away. Women are energized by expressing their feelings about what happened in their life. Men often don't understand how the mind of a woman works. Think of your wife's mind like a house that has five kids. They are all running around screaming, crying and acting out. To get peace in the house each child's needs must be properly care for. One put to bed, one given chores to do, one needs to get going on their homework and another put in the room by themselves so they can cool down. When all the kids are taken care of the house is quiet and peaceful.

That noisy house is what your wife's mind is like after either exciting or stressful things happen in her day. Her mind is running rampant like those five little children. The names of these rambunctious children causing havoc in her mind are: Concerns, Questions, Fears, Wild Thoughts and Frustration. They may also be named Joys, Ideas, Plans, Reports or Sharing. Both the good and bad things get your wife's mind going.

Just as you have to take care of the specific needs of your children before the house is quiet and peaceful, so the "children" running havoc or bouncing around in her mind won't calm down until each is expressed in conversation. The thoughts can be either the good things or concerns that she has. When Ed comes home Sue wants to tell him everything. Why does she want to do that? Because, in her mind, when experiences are shared or expressed he enters into her life and that quiets the commotion of the events of the day that are going through her mind. That is how Sue deals with her stresses, lingering thoughts, concerns and the joys of life. She has to express her thoughts or she will either get frustrated or not feel fulfilled or valued. She has to share them with him because communication builds relationships and fulfills her soul. When she shares these thoughts with him she now feels connected to him because he is now connected to the part of her day, i.e. her life, during which he was absent. Do you now have a better understanding of why communication is so needful and how that builds relationship?

If your wife is a stay at home mom who has small children, her need increases for adult conversation. She needs to enter the details of your day to connect with another adult so she doesn't feel so alone. This is how she connects with another adult. She wants you to fill her in on the details of your day so she can be part of your life. That is how she links up with you and feels connected in a relationship. Be sensitive to her need to hear the details of your life each day and value your opportunity to share your life with her. Then make sure you value her when she shares her day and life with you.

How Sex helps Him to Handle His Day

When it comes to sex Ed is very visual and he is easily excited. The thought of sex comes easily to his mind and won't leave, just as Sue's mind can't let go of her thoughts until they are expressed. He thinks about sex, and wants it, and he can imagine being with her and being close to her. How do you think Ed feels after anticipating being with Sue and then when he approaches her sensually she doesn't take him seriously? Or she dismisses his desires with a tone of voice that indicates that this is unimportant or childish or stupid? Sue found herself responding to Ed with reactions that were humiliating or demeaning in the way she pushed him away. One day it hit her that the way she was pushing Ed away made him feel he was not important to her at all. She realized something had to change immediately in the way she responded to him.

Just as Sue gets frustrated with Ed when he doesn't want to listen and talk; which can lead to depression for her, so Ed also gets equally frustrated but his response is anger because Sue rejects him and his advances. When she doesn't take his advances seriously in bed he reacts to her rejection by rolling over and this is the time that he starts to experience hurt feelings in his heart and frustration to her response. The next step is that anger starts to build up toward her. Sue has no idea Ed is reacting like that to her response because all is quiet in the bedroom. But you can cut that silence with a knife.

When Sue doesn't take Ed's needs seriously he gets angry and frustrated, and these feelings build up over time. There is, however something that Sue needs to recognize about Ed. When his sexual needs are met regularly, all the feelings of anger go away and for the most part he does not hold a grudge, and he does not bring those up in his thinking until there is a dry spell sexually. Men are not as complex as women. Some women will hold a grudge for his past failure for many years. When his needs are met then the issue that caused him anger and frustration is no longer a concern. A fulfilled man tends to go on with life, because most prefer a life of peace and fulfillment.

Sue's response to Ed's lack of communication is very similar to his feelings of rejection in the bedroom. When Ed does not feed her emotional needs or won't listen to her conversation Sue doesn't say anything. Unlike Ed she does not become angry because of his lack of sensitivity. Her usual response is more along the lines of disappointment in Ed, feelings of hurt or that she is unimportant. Then she feels cut off from him and then sadness takes over her inner being. Women of Sue's age have twice the propensity toward depression as do men. That means that sadness and hurt feed her depression every time he doesn't take communication seriously. Both have inner hurts that they seldom share with the other in open and non-confrontational communication

Getting back to Ed's need of sex, Sue does not comprehend just how important her responses are to him. His need for sex is a driving force in his life that needs to be met on a regular basis. Just because she doesn't think it is important or significant doesn't change the reality for Ed. What Sue fails to realize is what happens in Ed's thinking process when he feels consistently repeated rejections from his wife.

In the book "Every Man's Battle"[8] they address a man's physical need for sex. "*The human male, because of sperm production and other factors, naturally desires sexual release from every 48 to 72 hours. Many women, who especially in early-married life rarely have a matching level of desire, stand in amazement of how regularly their husbands desire sexual intercourse. But that's the way we are. If you're fortunate, your wife has developed a similar desire out of love for you (or out of pity!).*

How does the 72-hour cycle impact sexual purity of the eyes and mind? Watch yourself over the next couple of weeks. You have sex on Sunday night. Monday morning you drive to work and, without much reaction notice a new billboard with a foxy babe. But on your morning drive three sexless days later, seeing that babe gets your "motor" running, and she remains on your mind for miles. Later that day she occupies your thoughts during boring work meetings. The temptations may or may not intensify, but your sensitivity to them surely does. By the third day of the cycle, these temptations can seem cavernous."

This is something that Ed never thought of sharing with Sue. If she knew how Ed's thoughts and desires worked in his life she would probably respond differently to him. Never did she realize that his desires get more demanding and cavernous the longer they are left unattended by her. Because he seemed to be strong and independent Sue thought Ed could just deal with his desires and it was no big issue. When Sue learned this truth it opened her eyes to the importance of Ed's needs and she took her responsibility more seriously when he expressed his need for her. The more we understand why each has the needs they do, the better equipped we are to meet those needs with an understanding heart rather than a sarcastic response.

The Single-Focus Nature of a Man

One of the things you notice about men is their single focus. Sue tries talking with Ed when he is watching sports or his favorite program and she finds he is irritated or is unable to focus on her conversation.

When my girls were young sometimes they knew that if they wanted to talk to me when I was watching television that they would put their hands on both cheeks and turn my face toward them and say, "Dad I want to talk with you." I think they were being a bit melodramatic, but it did accomplish their purpose. We men can be single focused at times. The same is true when men are playing computer games, they are so focused they can't carry on a meaningful conversation with any one unless it is about the game. So this idea that men can turn everything else off and be single focused is not news to women. That truth was reinforced while watching an episode of the television program called "Big Bang Theory". The characters are all science nerds and they live across the hall from an attractive woman named Penny. The program focused on the four men's love of video game competition. They were playing Halo 4. At the end of the program they were in intense combat in their game when Penny walked in with three beautiful, sexy friends who she met while out dancing and asked the guys: "Do you guys all want to have sex with us?" They continued playing without batting an eye. They did not hear her because of their single focus. A moment later Leonard said, "Did you guys hear something?" They all looked pensive for a moment and said, "No" and they returned to their game. Men can turn everything off and be totally focused on one thing.

Sue needs to understand how a man's single focus plays out on the subject of sex. Ed gets Sue on his mind. He wants her and he needs her. He is thinking about being intimate with her. It is not enough that he grabs her once in a while. He wants to be fulfilled. He has a hard time focusing on anything else. (Remember his single focus.) He can be distracted for a while, but just like Sue's thoughts won't go away until they are expressed, so this single focused man has a single focused thought that does not go way until it is fulfilled. Sue doesn't realize how strong that desire is to Ed, and so when he approaches her, she may put him off, or she does not take his advances seriously because she is not in the mood. Maybe she just doesn't feel up to it right then. She may not think it is important to share her reasons with him about how specifically she is feeling so he can understand why she can't get into it right then, so instead of informing Ed, Sue just denies him. It is at this time that he truly feels rejected. Sue must come to understand this about Ed-- he is in his single focus mode and can't just turn off his desire.

That same single focus that was turned to Sue for sex is now turned inward and Ed experiences personal hurt, frustration, not feeling significant or not being important to her. When that goes on for extended times Ed then experiences anger over being rejected by his wife. When it happens continuously or long enough Sue will hear contempt in Ed's voice when talking about sex or he may make a comment off handedly declaring that she doesn't care about him or his needs. He may say it like he is joking, but that contempt for Sue may be very real. He may truly think that she doesn't care about him or his needs. She is hurting him and she doesn't seem to care, at least that is his perspective. How do you think that works in building a strong relationship? You can have all the meaningful conversation with him possible, but if he feels rejected by you when you turn him down for sex then meaningful conversation cannot bring him into deeper relationship with you until those needs are met.

Where do you want the single focus of your man to be? Having contempt for you in the way you are rejecting him or being content in the relationship in which he feels he is loved and cared for?

Understanding his urge in feminine terms

Nancy C. Anderson does a nice job of explaining the importance of a man's sexual needs in a way that women understand. She said:

47

"Ladies, have you ever gone on a PMS-driven mission called "Gotta have chocolate, or someone's gonna die"? I have. I once ransacked every drawer in my son's room looking for last year's semi-sweet Easter Bunny's ear. I've clawed through the kitchen cupboards like Indiana-Jones on a quest, looking for a little golden bag containing stale chocolate chips. As I ripped it open and blissfully inhaled the aroma, my pulse reacted as if I'd just found the necklace that the old lady threw off the Titanic.

Now imagine that you're on a take-no-prisoners chocolate chase and your husband has a Snickers bar in his locked briefcase—but he won't give you the key. He has the capability to relieve your hormonal obsession, but he refuses. How would you feel about him? Would you think that he was selfish? Mean? Cruel? That's how a man feels when his wife rejects his sexual needs."[9]

If Sue does not meet Ed's needs, what do you think she expects him to do? Suppress it? When she thinks that way she makes him vulnerable to sexual thoughts and fantasies. It becomes harder for Ed to deal with the many temptations he faces around him. So many women dress provocatively these days with the express intent of catching a man's eye. Porn is a click away on the internet and the women there are inviting men to enjoy them and they are so eager and happy to have men watch. If Ed does such things and Sue finds out, she will get very angry and hurt that he is not being faithful to her. But then again she didn't take his needs seriously. (I am not justifying porn by this statement; I'm simply recognizing that is the motivation of why some may respond that way.) A man doesn't get married to live a celibate life. Another fall-out from a man watching porn is that he may develop an even higher expectation of sexual fulfillment from his wife and some come to a place where they aren't attracted to her any more. It is not right for the man to engage in porn or to lust after provocatively dressed women. It is wrong and there is no justification for it. On the other hand it is also wrong for the wife to withhold herself from fulfilling his legitimate sexual needs that he has.

Turning to Fantasy

Since the subject of porn was raised in the last section, let me make some observations about how we compensate when our needs are not being met. When we don't have what we need, we tend to look for an alternative and usually an inferior method in which to satisfy that need. It becomes a substitute for the real thing. Even though sex is not all of what a relationship is about, it is a very important element to a growing, meaningful relationship. Even though a woman's need for emotional connection is not all that a relationship is about, it is a very important element of it. Let's take this opportunity to focus on how a couple might turn to the world of fantasy when the reality of their relationship is not being met by the other.

When a man's sexual needs are not met some may seek fulfillment through pornography. Porn is nothing but fantasy about a mythical woman. Think about why he might engage his thoughts in porn.

-She is not there for him as frequently as he desires.

-She is not making advances to him or initiating sex and he equates that to her having no interest in him.

-He feels she is not valuing him or respecting his needs.

-What do some men do when she consistently refuses his legitimate sexual desires? Many seek out satisfaction for a release from that tension through porn.

-The women on porn sites are young, exciting and always available whenever he has a need.

-They want him (well, at least that is the impression they give).

-They will do whatever he wants and if this one doesn't the next one will.

-She comes across as one who wants and enjoys sex in a voracious way all the time.

-They portray themselves as being willing to do anything to satisfying him.

-She knows how visual he is and so she will dress provocatively, exhibit herself to lure him or tease him in the way she slowly undresses so he will anticipate her.

-She will do anything she can think of to attract his attention and satisfy his sensual needs.

When he gets hooked on porn, how can you compete with these young, perfectly proportioned, hard-bodied women? But that which drives him is his desire to have his unmet needs met. Again, I am not condoning this kind of action, but simply stating what goes on in many men's lives when they view porn. Also, please remember that porn is all fantasy. It is not real life. Even though he is responsible for his own choices and actions, make sure you are not contributing to his problem through your neglect. Don't give him reason to take refuge in the porn world.

What I have just said is very difficult for many women to comprehend, so before I go on and address the woman's fantasy world, it is important that you take a reality check about what you have just read. Many women tend to deal with strong feelings of inferiority when a relationship goes to a comparison level. It is easy to think you are in a competition because you are not as beautiful or as thin or as young as some of those women he is looking at on the porn websites.

Always keep in mind that fantasies are just lies wrapped up in beautiful packages that we love to believe. When unwrapped they are less than reality. The truth of the matter is that he chose you as his wife. You are the only person with whom he can have sex without guilt. He needs you to satisfy him. As much as you think that good looks and body size is the most important thing, you need to recognize that if your man is a good willed man that it is pretty much true that if you are consistently there for him you will meet his needs and he will be satisfied. You can't minimize the importance of sex with your husband in your relationship like you have in the past. Let him enjoy you and don't withhold yourself because you don't feel beautiful or because you think you are lacking in some way. When a man's needs are met he tends to be content where he is. Your marriage is worth working on.

According to a report by the National Marriage Project at the University of Virginia, contrary to what you hear in the media, sex can be very good and satisfying in marriage, and people who are married tend to enjoy more good sex than single people or cohabitating couples. I share this to encourage you to work on this area of your relationship to make your marriage better and to keep it strong.

In the published report on the "National Marriage Project" the University of Virginia writes:

"Contrary to the popular belief that married sex is boring and infrequent, married people report higher levels of sexual satisfaction than both sexually active singles and cohabiting couples, according to the most comprehensive and recent survey of sexuality. Forty-two percent of wives said that they found sex extremely emotionally and physically satisfying, compared to just 31 percent of single women who had a sex partner. And 48 percent of husbands said sex was extremely satisfying emotionally, compared to just 37 percent of cohabiting men. The higher level of commitment in marriage is probably the reason for the high level of reported sexual satisfaction; marital commitment contributes to a greater sense of trust and security, less drug and alcohol-infused sex, and more mutual communication between the couple."[10]

I share this because when people stop believing in the importance of marriage they tend to give up in their willingness to improve what they have. Even though your husband has messed up, it is worth the effort to work through the problem and to make every aspect of your marriage better. Rebuilt marriages can be stronger because they know what they need and they work to strengthen those areas in order to develop a more meaningful relationship.

Okay ladies, before we look at your fantasy life, let me note a statistic I read. "One out of every six women struggles with an addiction to pornography." It's getting to not just be a man thing anymore. If it is wrong for men it is also wrong for women.

The focus of women's fantasy is different. Where does a woman turn when her emotional and communication needs are not being fulfilled? She is frustrated because she is not finding emotional fulfillment from her husband who is like a brick when it comes to communication and meaningful emotional exchanges. Where can she go to find life that is exciting and fulfilling and still stay married? She turns to a more socially acceptable source than pornography. She enters the fantasy world of romance novels and chick-flicks to fill her soul. What may characterize her man?

-He does not listen to her.
-He is not there for her emotionally.
-He does not take her needs seriously.

-He is not making her feel special in any way.
-He is not sharing his life with her in meaningful ways.
-He seems to focus only on his own world and doesn't take her needs
 seriously.

To fulfill her own needs she turns to fantasy. She brings men into her life vicariously through the main character of the novel or movie. Think about how this happens.

-When she starts reading the romance novel she puts herself in the
 place of the woman portrayed.
-She meets a man and he sweeps her off her feet.
-He notices everything about her.
-He is taken by her beauty and friendliness.
-He is there to cater to her most significant needs and helps her face
 her fears.
-There is romance in what they talk about and where he takes her.
-He listens to her and together they explore each other's thoughts and
 feelings.
-After he has fully engaged her through intimate conversation and they
 are making love he fulfills her every time and she is passionate in
 those sweet encounters.
-He will risk life and limb to save her from the danger that is pursuing
 her. He will do anything for her

These are the kinds of things that grab her heart. The more she reads these romance novels and watches the chick flicks and thinks about them the more unrealistic her expectations are of her husband. The very same kind of thing that the wayward husband experienced in his fantasy life is what she indulges in for herself. Yet when you talk about it in public it is so much more acceptable. Is fantasy thinking any more right for her than it is for him?

I am not seeking to justify the action of either but seeking to make the point of what really is happening. We have to see the big picture here and not get bogged down with needless detail that will take us nowhere. *Here is the principal issue*. When a person's needs are not met by the other then they become vulnerable and the fantasy world is where they tend to retreat. In this fantasy world everything they desire in a relationship is met by someone other than their spouse. Their fantasy world gives them the adventure and experience in which their imaginary or seemingly available person is giving them the full devotion that their mate is not giving them any longer. In their dream world this fantasy person caters to their whims, doing those things that make them feel important, fulfilled and significant, and they never tire of meeting their needs. Their fantasy world gives them everything they desire in an ideal relationship that they are not experiencing in real life with their real spouse, in the real world. Now they have an expectation that their spouse could never fulfill. How much do you withdraw to this fantasy world in your night dreams and day dreams?

The question is this: **Do you want a fantasy relationship or a real relationship?** It doesn't take much discipline or risk of making yourself vulnerable, nor does it require courage of facing up to those sticky issues of life to live in your imaginary world. Are you seeking refuge in your fantasies instead of in the reality of your relationship? It takes time, thought and hard work to understand another person and their needs in order to develop a meaningful relationship. You can't pursue a real relationship if you are living in the fantasy world that leaves you with unrealistic expectations that your spouse can't meet.

It is easy to take pot-shots at the other person because they indulge in a fantasy world of porn or romance novels. Maybe the reason you are taking shots at your spouse is because you don't want to accept personal responsibility in learning how to be there for them. As soon as we start to condemn the other person to their face we become their accuser, and thus, we feel superior to them. We tend to look down on them, and a meaningful, growing relationship is never built from such a perspective. Marriage is about relationship between equals and being willing to pay the price to not just be there for the other, but to help them mature so they can reach their full potential. Marriage is for adults willing to take on adult responsibilities in a real world. I hope you are willing to pay the price for this worthwhile treasure.

Initiate

Edward and Susan went to a fancy restaurant to eat dinner one evening. They were having a quiet conversation while waiting for the waitress to come take the order. After a while they noticed that she hadn't come in to take even their beverage order yet. People who were seated after them had their drinks and their order was taken already and they still had no contact with their waitress. Ed noticed this all the while they were talking and he started to get irritated over the lack of service and he was becoming more distant from Susan. Finally he got the attention of their waitress and told her they hadn't been waited on yet. She said, I'm busy but I'll get back with you. Others were getting their food around them and Ed was getting more irritated. They had been there for forty five minutes and the only contact they had with the waitress was when Ed got her attention to inform her that they were still waiting. When an hour passed Ed was even more distraught and he said to Susan, "Let's get out of here!" He was not a happy camper, and they got up and left the restaurant.

Why was Ed upset? The answer is obvious; the waitress had not initiated contact with them to take their order. The waitress' lack of attention declared that they were not important to *her* and they could just wait until it was convenient for *her*. They had expectation of reasonable service and she had not even made an effort. The result is that as they left they declared they would never give their business to that restaurant anymore. Can you blame them?

This little story has a great deal to do with the section on fantasy we just finished. Why does Sue get frustrated when she always finds herself looking for ways to get Ed to take time to talk with her, meet her emotional needs and take care of things around the house? She wants Ed to voluntarily share what happened in his day and to take an interest in what went on in her day. Sue wants Ed to take out the trash without being told, and to do those repairs she has talked about without being reminded a hundred times. She wants Ed to remember those birthdays and anniversaries and to take the lead in planning some of the special events without prompting or reminding. In other words she needs Ed to initiate action and conversation to show how much he cares. The reason Sue would get involved in the romance novels and chick flicks is because he wasn't going out of his way to make her feel special. He focused on things that interested him but did not initiate meeting her needs. Fantasy was her way of feeling someone cared about her and made her feel special.

The same is true from Ed's perspective. Sue would be there for him in many ways, but she seldom initiated intimate times with him, and because she was tired or involved in something else she thought intimacy like kissing hugging or touching was not all that important. She would be there for him when he needed sex, and her thought was that he should be satisfied with that. What Sue did not realize was that Ed needed her to show him that he is important to her. He needed her to initiate intimacy, and sexual contact. When Sue realized how important it was for her to initiate in these areas to meet his needs she talked with Ed about what he needed from her. From there they established what she felt comfortable doing and the frequency and that helped her fulfill his needs so he didn't feel like he was unimportant to her. That is how Ed needed Susan to express her love for him.

People seek out fantasy because the other has taken them for granted; they have stopped initiating the meaningful contact with their spouse. They recognize their own needs, but neglect to show love by initiating actions that seek to fulfill the needs of the other.

Think about this, your wife goes to the famous restaurant called **"Fulfilled Needs"**. You are the waiter and you are going about your daily routine of work, hobbies, talking on the phone, working on the computer. Your wife is waiting at the table for you to take her order. Have you been ignoring her or have you initiated taking her request for the needs she wants fulfilled by you? Since you are the waiter it is your task to initiate the order to understand her needs so you can meet them. Are you like the waitress in the opening scene that is too busy with everybody else to pay attention to all her customers? Or will you be a good waiter and initiate the contact to find out what your wife's needs are so you can serve her?

Even though the husband's responsibility is the focus of the above illustration, the wife needs to put herself into the story as being the waitress waiting on her husband. She too must initiate meeting his needs just as he should be committed to initiating actions to meet her needs. Relationship is a two way street.

Synonyms for the word initiate are: "commence; introduce, launch." It is putting into action your ideas and concerns. It's learning what the other needs and doing something about it. Instead of fretting that the other has not been meeting your needs, commit yourself to initiate meeting the needs the other has. As time goes on you will notice the different attitude the other has to you. Don't be hesitant to take the opportunity to let them know exactly what you need from them. They may be more open to your requests because of the way you have been treating them. Marriage is about mutually seeking the betterment of the other person and you can't do that without serving them. Serving means that you learn their needs and initiate action.

Women Struggle with Loneliness

Do you recognize the loneliness that your spouse experiences? Mary Whelchel states in her article titled ***Dealing with Loneliness***[11]: *"Someone has said that "All man's history is an endeavor to shatter his loneliness." We are designed by God for fellowship, for companionship and when it is missing, it affects our motivation, our self-respect, our happiness–almost every part of our lives."* Loneliness is a big deal to both men and women. Mother Teresa said "Loneliness and the feeling of being unwanted is the most terrible poverty." That poverty is found in many marriages because the needs of one or both spouses continue to go unmet in so many different ways. All the while they may not be able to put a finger on what they are experiencing even though that is a great emptiness in their life that they seek to fill.

It seems strange that we can experience loneliness in a crowded room, but none the less true. In a marriage where each ought to be there for the other and help alleviate some of the source of loneliness it can actually become more acute when you feel unimportant because the person is making no attempt to be there for you. Even though the person is right there with you, it seems like, on various levels, you have a lingering feeling of isolation in your soul. That which makes loneliness so intense is the associated feeling of rejection. Have you noticed such feelings as isolation and rejection are associated with loneliness? Someone said "Loneliness is everything it's cracked up to be." How true!

Women feel loneliness on various fronts. Communication in their marriage relationship is their major front. When I talk with married women about their loneliness the first place they go is to their husband, whom they say does not know how to communicate with them or meet their emotional needs. Why do they go there? Because he has not connected with her and the result is that she feels lonely and empty. If a woman is lonely long enough then the depression, with which she struggles, will intensify. Why are some women so busy? They never seem to have the house clean enough or they have to be doing something with their hands, such as knitting or doing some craft project. These things can be a distraction from their loneliness and boredom in order to fill their void and keep their sanity.

When Sue feels that she is not connecting to Ed it fuels her loneliness. Her deep feelings of loneliness come because she thinks that Ed doesn't care, or if he does try to care it is only a surface concern, for he really doesn't care enough to meet her needs. It seems like Ed cares only about himself and his own satisfaction. Sue thinks that her needs are actually secondary to fulfilling his own and she doesn't feel important in his eyes.

A women's loneliness can be caused by many different reasons, but the longing of her heart is to feel connected, valued and loved. She gets married to the man with whom she connected and who was so interested in her before marriage, but many find that after marriage the fountain of conversation dries up and the loneliness starts to haunt her.

Ed likes to solve problems, fix things and understand complicated issues. He came to realize that his challenge is to understand his wife's need of communication and how he can do something about it. He decided that the best course of action is to research this topic so he can understand how Sue could feel satisfied in the area of communication in their relationship. He found some good books to help him understand how he can improve his communication and meet Sue's needs. The male desire to "fix things" motivate him to work on a "fix" for improving their relationship. He wanted to make sure he was doing everything he could to make Susan feel fulfilled and connected to him so her loneliness is dispelled.

Men Struggle with Loneliness

John Steinbeck's novel, *Of Mice and Men[12]*, *has a quote that says: 'A guy needs somebody-to be near him.' He whined, 'A guy goes nuts if he ain't got nobody.'"* This reminds us that as strong as men seem they too struggle with loneliness, a profound sense of loneliness.

Most women don't know that men struggle with loneliness. Men usually don't wear their emotions on their sleeves for others to see. They keep it buried and suppressed lest the world see their vulnerability. In the same way women feel loneliness when they don't connect through communication, so men feel loneliness when they don't connect on a regular basis with their wives physically or sexually. You might be tempted to say that he only wants to be connected physically. But if you think that then you are wrong. They want their women to be involved in their adventure of life. He wants her to be by his side in the things he enjoys doing; to cheer him on, to be his partner. Loneliness is a monster that he faces and he is left to the mercy of his wife to help slay that foe. This point is made most powerfully in the first of the four points that are quoted from Shaunti Feldhahn in chapter two about the loneliness men experience when talking about the need men have for sex. *(It can be found three paragraphs into the chapter, first point)*

Ed experienced deep hurts from Sue over the years. He feels it deeply when she rejects his advances, or when she doesn't think he is important enough to give herself freely to him or initiate sex more frequently. Sue is thinking that because she is just not in the mood it is alright to say no. It never crosses her mind that she is rejecting him in any way, after all she loves him, and that should never be questioned. However, that is not how it comes across to Ed. Why is he so vulnerable when he feels rejected? It is because the perceived rejection from Sue deepens his sense of loneliness. When he is connected with Sue it quiets that monster of loneliness in his soul.

If you don't think that sense of loneliness is strong in a man you only need to watch him after he breaks up, divorces or experiences the death of a spouse. Within twelve to eighteen months after a death or divorce many men are already dating and ready to get married. When he breaks up he will seek another girlfriend as soon as possible. When men don't have a woman in their life many are aimless and their loneliness intensifies. Statistics say that anywhere from 65-75 percent of men remarry after a divorce or death of a spouse. These are strong indications that men can't stand to be alone. Men are *very* vulnerable to their loneliness just as women are. It is not always as obvious in men for many just cover their loneliness better than women. Men tend to be more aggressive in seeking out someone.

The deepest need of the heart is to belong to someone, to be in relationship, to be important to another and to feel connected. When such needs are not met it leaves a person empty and they feel lonely, yes, intensely lonely. We were not meant to feel prolonged separation in a marriage relationship, yet sometimes marriage is the loneliest place on earth. There may not be any tell-tale signs of their loneliness at first, or they may not express it in a blatant manner, but it is there, hiding under the surface.

If you listen to what they are saying they will give you clues. If you are deaf to their clues the depth of their loneliness will be expressed in other ways, such as more boldness in their criticism of you, sadness, depression, anger or becoming more distant. You can only blow up a balloon so far for it to be safe. If you continue to add more air it will eventually explode. A person's soul is also like a balloon in that they can take only so much loneliness, rejection, and hurt before it harms their personality or it kills the marriage and makes being together very lonely. Conversation will starve your wife's loneliness and sex will asphyxiate your husband's loneliness. Your calling as a man or woman is to get more involved and do all you can to slay that monster called Loneliness that resides in the soul of your mate.

The Bible has something significant to say about Sex in Marriage

The Bible is God's instruction book on how to deal with our existence and offers much wisdom for every area of life. God initiates marriage as well as sex before sin entered the world according to Genesis 2:18-25. In talking about sex in one passage it addresses the importance of sex needing to be in the marriage relationship. 1 Corinthians 7:2-5 says:

"But, because of sexual immoralities, let each man have his own wife, and let each woman have her own husband. Let the husband render to his wife the affection owed her, and likewise also the wife to her husband. The wife doesn't have authority over her own body, but the husband. Likewise also the husband doesn't have authority over his own body, but the wife. Don't deprive one another, unless it is by consent for a season, that you may give yourselves to fasting and prayer, and may be together again, that Satan doesn't tempt you because of your lack of self-control."[13]

There are many important teachings here but notice three significant points in this passage.

1. Our bodies do not belong to ourselves in marriage. We are to think about the needs of the other.
2. The second says *"Don't deprive one other."* That means sex is not to be withheld from the other for it is rightfully due them in the relationship.
3. The final is a warning that if the couple doesn't come together sexually that they become vulnerable to greater temptation. When

we do our part to fulfill their deepest need we protect them from their vulnerabilities. This says your concern is not to be limited to your own needs but also to the needs of your spouse. Marriage is not about just our own needs being met, but being committed to being there for the other.

The woman's need of honest communication and the man's need of sexual fulfillment with his wife are legitimate needs that must be taken seriously in the marriage relationship if you want to experience growth and closeness. Don't deprive each other of what they most need for that makes them vulnerable to loneliness and rejection or feeling unloved or unimportant.

Chapter Four: It's all in the Mind

Earlier Nancy C. Anderson expressed the importance of sex to a man, but did not explain why. To understand another reason why your husband needs sex is very important. It may even help you understand why his sexual need must be met before your need for deeper and more meaningful communication can be addressed by him. Recognize there are times he is incapable of opening up in communication until his needs have been met by you.

Your mind on Chemicals

When both men and women face pressure in life there is a stress chemical that is released at an increased rate in the brain called cortisol. Every one of us experiences the frustration of stress from negative emotions and knows how, over time, it weighs heavily on our mind. To have continual, prolonged stress, and not deal with it could, potentially, cause depression and other health problems.

In your home you can handle the cleanup of the daily tracking in of dirt through your kitchen, but if your husband sprinkled a fine layer of soot all over your kitchen floor every day it would soon have far reaching effects all over the house. If you don't clean it up right away it gets tracked into other areas of the house and even onto your furniture. It becomes harder to keep everything clean. If he does this every day without it being cleaned your problems spread further and more intensely throughout your house.

In the same way if your husband does not gain release from his stress, cortisol builds up the next day and becomes more pronounced and more intense. Just like the soot in your kitchen is tracked all over the house, so the soot of the stress that produces cortisol spreads all over his being and takes greater control. It affects his attitudes, his sense of peace, his outlook on life, his ability to freely communicate, and if it lasts long enough it can have a negative effect on his health. Let me add that the effects of cortisol are also just as true for women as well.

All stress is not bad, but unresolved stress over long periods continues to build up cortisol and it brings about a negative impact on one's health and emotional well being. During these times of unresolved stress and the build-up of cortisol it is not unusual for the man to shut down his communication and become depressed. He is not as free or able to open up when cortisol builds. That is the nature of cortisol as it builds up from the stress and pressures of life. Just because he doesn't show depression or a lack of well being openly like you do, doesn't mean it is not there. It's just affecting him differently. Men tend to bury their feelings. Have you ever wondered why he comes home and wants to veg out for a while before talking or doing anything else? Relaxing helps him wind down. Do you know why he can't handle hearing about all the details of your day at that time? The stresses of his day (and maybe several days) have caused levels of cortisol to take their toll on him. It suppresses his ability to freely communicate with you.

Do you enjoy those times after sex when you really connected and both of you just talk about everything? During this time you both are so open and talk so freely and maybe you can't even shut him up at times. Do you know why sex opens him up, or maybe gives him a release in his spirit that is so noticeable? It has to do with two other chemicals that are released in the brain during sex. It is Oxytocin and vasopressin. These are chemicals that also help reduce the levels of cortisol. Oxytocin positively impacts the desire for communication while vasopressin helps to lower the male's negative behavior during communication. Endorphins produce a general sense of well-being, including feeling soothed, peaceful and secure. Such endorphins are released during sex.

That is why a man can feel stress free and open with you after sex. Because he feels soothed, peaceful and secure, he tends to open up and feel that everything is all right. You may notice in the movies that a spy will often open up to a call girl. He has little or no history with her, but he does have a pleasant time with her which culminates with sex. He will open up to her after sex because he feels secure and therefore able to share the struggles and even those secrets he has to keep hidden from everyone else. It is the same with your husband. After sex he is then able to open up and communicate with you because the oxytocin neutralized the effects of cortisol. It's like he is set free from the bondage of cortisol. He feels freer to interact, ready to go to work the next day and take on the new challenges with renewed vigor.

You have a powerful influence over your husband. Just realize that he may not be able to open up with you *until* he has had sex. His desire for sex is his expression to connect with you and to be able to open up with you. Sex is an important key that unlocks your husband emotionally. If you don't believe it, give your husband sex freely for a week or two, even be aggressive and initiate it and see how that affects his ability and willingness to open up with you. If you are hesitating to do what I just mentioned, then you need to ask yourself why are you are playing games with your relationship by withholding that which your husband needs so desperately.

I was listening to a counselor speaker many years ago, it was while I was in college, and he was saying that one of the things a wife could do to encourage her husband through any trauma that comes into his life, such as a job loss, financial downturn, difficult times at work, etc., was to have good sex with him. He spoke of the renewed ability the husband would have to be able to deal with those difficulties he faced. I heard this truth many years before all of the research that transpired on the mapping of the brain. Brain mapping just helps us to understand what part of the brain controls the various functions of your body as well as reactions to life around you.

You may not understand why men act and react like they do, but what is imperative is that you know why sex is important to a man. When you know that sex can free him up so he can communicate, you then know how to be there for him and your thoughtful response will make a world of difference that will strengthen your relationship. You are that important to him. This is why men will fight for their woman or become jealous if she flirts because she is his companion and the source of his ability to function in life as well as the one he connects with in a meaningful relationship. Don't minimize what is so important to him.

Helping your wife

Women struggle with depression. Before females reach puberty they have the same frequency of depression as do males. Starting around age fourteen their frequency doubles that of men. After menopause the rate reduces to about the same for women and men. During those in between years they battle with depression. As I thought about cortisol's negative effect on the woman's brain I asked myself a question; "Is there something a man can do to help her deal with her depression in the way he treats her or interacts with her?" There are various causes of depression, but if her cause of depression is from cortisol and not other hormones, then what can he do to help her?

If you want to learn more about how oxytocin is produced as well as how it affects you then you can find more information in Addendum 1. There are specific triggers that stimulate the excretion of oxytocin and that helps to neutralize the affects of cortisol. Meaningful sex is one of the stimulations for the secretion of Oxytocin in your brain; but that is not the only trigger. Notice also in the Addendum that humor as well as a good relationship with your spouse and the feeling of belonging also triggers the release of Oxytocin. Luanne Brizendine adds to that list by identifying other triggers such as touching, gazing, positive emotional interaction, hugging and kissing, and sexual orgasm that activates the release of oxytocin in the female brain.

Men like the idea of sex being the answer, but notice some of the other triggers. Humor, means there is some light heartedness in the relationship instead of constantly picking on each other, making fun of the other or thinking the worst about them in what they do. Set a positive tone in your relationship. Relax and enjoy life together in a good non-threatening way. Don't make everything an issue. The positive effect will produce more than a pleasant setting in which to live life.

Good relationship and positive emotional interaction is next on our list. Have you asked what that looks like to her? Does she need you to listen to her more or for you to share more of your life with her? Does she need more romance and uninterrupted, meaningful time with you? She needs you to value what she says by listening and interacting with her. It includes a sense of well being in your relationship by you keeping your word as you follow through on your promises and responsibilities, and working out your differences instead of stonewalling her or not taking her needs seriously. She wants you to maintain a growing respectful relationship with her.

Whereas sex is what helps free him from the damaging effects of cortisol, regular, meaningful communication and positive emotional interaction is what she needs to help free her from the damaging effects of cortisol which can cause her depression. She doesn't think of sex as often as you do because most of the time she does not have the consistent climax that a man does that produces oxytocin. That which is more powerful to her is found in meaningful relationship, and

65

emotional interaction. Just as you want her to understand and meet your needs, so, in the same way, you have to be just as concerned about understanding and meeting her needs. That which also counteracts the damaging effects of cortisol and increases her level of oxytocin and which brings her calmness and peace of mind is not being met through the needed meaningful communication, emotional interaction and relationship with her husband.

Women, to help yourself, you need to understand how to unlock your husband so he can open up to you. The earlier teaching on instructing your husband why communication is so important to you and how he can be there for you must be built into your relationship. The more he enters into your life through meaningful conversation the more likely you are to be freed from depression caused by cortisol. I realize there are other causes of depression, including physical problems and relationship struggles in life, family problems, and life pressures as well as monthly cycles. There are many women who are emotionally sick because their husbands won't listen to them, or share with them, or talk about their problems or let them into their lives. She lives to connect with him and when that doesn't happen in significant ways that is a major stress that builds up her cortisol level. When he is not there for her then she doesn't feel fulfilled or connected. When he does connect with her then that helps produce the oxytocin which gives her a sense of well being in the relationship. Over time her frustration of not being fulfilled will bring on depression and often deep depression as she longs for that fulfilling relationship that isn't coming her way. If he belittles the detail of her conversation and refuses to listen to her she feels a little more distant every day and feels like she is being sucked into a black hole of meaninglessness.

To be there for her, he must learn how to let her into his life through sharing events of his day, as well as sharing his dreams, concerns, fears, joys and struggles. She may not always be ready to have sex but she can decide to be there for him so his needs can be met. In the same way he needs to be there for her by listening, interacting and learning how to engage with her in meaningful conversations. He will allow her to talk and he will take a genuine interest in what she is saying, if for no other reason than she needs you to show that you truly care about her. You don't want your wife to minimize your need for sex, so you must never minimize or humiliate her because of her need to share thoughts and the details of her stories. Meeting needs is a two way street that must be traveled by each.

You might want to do your own "clinical trial" and see how the level of your wife's depression changes when you both engage in meaningful exchanges on a regular basis and do special things with each other. Just as sex frees you from your stresses, so getting away from stressful situations on a special date frees her as well. When she asks about your day, pick one or two significant things and tell her about it with some of the detail. How long might it take for this to affect your wife? Plan on doing it every day for at least three to six months and notice the effects in her demeanor.

I was talking with a woman from our church whose mother recently died. Her parents were married 68 years. She told about them sitting around every morning after breakfast for at least an hour and just talking. He had learned the secret of listening and taking part in good conversation with her and it was very fulfilling for both of them. I don't imagine this was something natural for him at first, but over the years he learned how to do this. It may be a long learning experience for you, but if you value your wife you will set aside time regularly where she has your full attention and you will learn to open up and enjoy this dimension of your relationship

Perhaps you thought that my suggestion for working on conversation for three to six months was a long time. Remember that is just for the purpose of seeing if the level of her depression changes. The need of such communication is for a life time. Wouldn't it be great that you would both be enjoying each other fully on your sixtieth anniversary as well? Of course you may have to talk a little louder then and maybe you will miss some of the conversation often, but you will know that the other cares.

My Story

I want to share my story that relates to the importance of the previous section. I was hindered for several months in publishing this book because I was waiting for permission from publishers to quote their works. During that time of waiting we discovered that my wife had a very aggressive form of cancer with only twelve to eighteen months to live. Sadly we found out that she only had one month. Our time over that last couple of months had a lot of tears and was filled with talks about everything dear and important to us. We grew so close to each other and enjoy each our time tremendously. There was such a great freedom to talk openly about our feelings and concerns. Along with our faith this teaching helped us deal with this difficult time with great calmness and peace of heart.

67

I started out in marriage without being much of a conversationalist or knowing how to share my feelings. My focus was on my work which demanded a lot of my time. But one thing I did that I didn't realize was so important was that I continued to date my wife. I usually spent my day off with her and we always took vacations together. We had a consistent time with each other that gave us opportunity to talk about all kinds of things that were on our minds or in our lives. I spent 39 years in a profession in which my wife was a very active part of my work. We would talk about the people we were involved with, the new programs we were developing, but also we talked about our children, looked forward to and planned our vacations every year. It took me a lot of years to come to enjoy my time of conversation with Nancy.

We were going through one of those rough patches in our life and Nancy and I hadn't had our date time for a few weeks and I found myself missing our conversations. I felt empty. I hadn't felt that way before about needing time with Nancy to just talk and catch up. I realized how much our talk-times meant to me and how fulfilling they were. We had learned that art of communication by sharing what is important to us, and what our concerns are and what we were looking forward to in our life and work. That did more than just meet Nancy's needs, but I discovered at that point that an area of my life had been developed and was being nourished by our talk-times together.

Just because a couple lives together for thirty or forty years doesn't mean they have developed a deep relationship that nourishes each other. Since my retirement I have become a hospice chaplain. I go into homes and talk with the families of people who are dying. As a person comes closer to death they tend to sleep more and so my time is often focused more on family members. Recently I was talking with a woman who had been married 45 years and she was telling me that she wished that when her husband was awake that he could emotionally relate to her and the kids. He had never learned to open up and verbally share himself and his love for his family. I'm not questioning his love; I'm just saying that some people never learn how to effectively get involved in a meaningful way in the lives of those they love. I've heard so many children say that they wished they would hear their father say that he loves them and appreciates what they have accomplished in life. Deeper communication that knows how to meet the emotional needs of the other is learned through practice rather than just being with a person for a long time. Even if you love the other person, such static love is not enough to fulfill them and their emotional needs. Love needs to be shown, vocalized and expressed. Love is an action verb that motivates us to seek the betterment of another; it is not a noun, that is, a thing we possess like an object.

It is because I took time over the years to learn how to share my thoughts and express emotional needs that my wife and I enjoyed deeper levels of communication. We talked about her death and about how our children and grandchildren would deal with this tragic announcement. We talked about our friends and their involvement in our lives. We reminisce about our life, our work, our children and friends. We talked about the things we wished we could still do and the anticipated joys of life like the growth of our grandchildren. We talked about what she wanted in her funeral and who she wanted to speak at it. We talked about her pain and wondered together about her process of dying. We discussed the reality of heaven and what it would be like and what it will be like to stand in the presence of her Savior. Some of the topics were deep and sensitive and others were concerns, and still others were the fun times we enjoyed. We were able to speak freely and openly because we learned to be candid with each other and allow the other to speak what was on their mind without it becoming a major issue of offense or debate each time. It was while writing this book that so many lights went on in my understanding about the dynamics of our relationship and why giving details of my day and thoughts were so important to my wife. The writing of this book is an expression of my passion to help couples understand each other and be able to develop a deeper relationship because of this information.

If you think that deep communication is just going to happen because you have been together for so long, then you are going to have a rude awaking when you find yourself living with a stranger after the kids leave. Communication is something that has to be worked on, developed and encouraged. There are times when it is very fragile and your cruel comments, your sarcastic tone, your thoughtless or rude words will crush the life out of your mate's willingness to open up with you to share what is on their heart. One of the reasons so many marriages fail after seven to eight years is because healthy communication has not been developed on which to build a strong and lasting relationship. This quality is not built by passivity but by active involvement in her life. If you make this need in her life a priority now, then you will find that it will yield greater dividends as you grow old together.

Go ahead, Make His Day!

Louann Brizendine in her book "The Female Brain" says: *"In both males and females, oxytocin causes relaxation, fearlessness, bonding and contentment with each other. Oxytocin is not only stimulated by sexual orgasm but also stimulated by closeness and touch. Males need to be touched two to three times more frequently than females to maintain the same level of oxytocin. Without frequent touch when mates are apart, the brain's dopamine and oxytocin circuits and receptors can feel starved. Oxytocin draws people together for pleasure, comfort and calm."*[14]

You start to comprehend the importance of the above quote when you think about your relationship and how you have been responding to each other. Why does he want to hug, kiss and touch you? Why is it so important to cuddle? Why is a passionate kiss, when one of you comes home, something you think of as unimportant now? You enjoyed it when you were dating. Maybe you are not in the mood for romance, and you don't want such passion to end up in the bedroom. You may be tired of those pointless or insignificant touches that come all too often, from your perspective. Recognizing those touches as his way of feeling close or bonded to you can give you the understanding to properly respond to them instead of reacting with a snide or belittling comment of disgust. He needs that touch to feel bonded to you, and even though talking fulfills your needs it does not fulfill that inner need for him at that time.

His touch is a declaration to you that he needs you to feel whole, and to criticize that is to belittle his most important, and let me say legitimate need that he is experiencing. That need is real. His oxytocin circuits and receptors feel starved and are stimulated with your touches and his touching of you. This calms him, and it draws him closer to you. More than likely he doesn't realize why this is so important to him; he just knows he has that need. If you criticize him and push him away that shuts down his desire to want to open up and talk. If you respond with a negative response you are not respecting what is important to him. The distance he feels from your denial increases each time you reject him or his advances. If you add attitude to your response that increases the intensity of rejection he feels from you.

What do you think your response will be the next time he greets you and wants to touch you and hold you and kiss you? There was a time you

70

really enjoyed that, but now do you put up a defense because you are not in the mood? Do you get fearful that if you respond like he wants that you will end in the bedroom and you are just not in the mood? Or will you enjoy him and let him enjoy you for a moment before you get on with what you were doing, telling him he will just have to wait till later? Say those words with a twinkle in your eyes and you will have his full attention. You are just as responsible as he is to not let the romance escape from your marriage. Continue to have fun with each other and it will keep your marriage vibrant.

The Twenty Seconds Rule

In Louann Brizendine's book she says that holding each other for twenty seconds releases oxytocin which is the bonding agent in relationships.[15] Twenty seconds is a minimum, so is he worth a minute of your time? Is she worth a minute of your time once or twice a day? Is strengthening your relationship worth a minute of your time? Both of you need these bonding times every day. There is a part of the brain that feels starved and you are the "feast" that satisfies their inner being; you are the "Valium" that quiets and calms the restlessness of their mind and soul. Are you willing to feed your mate's soul each day and bring them calm?

Let me encourage you to read the above quote by Brizendine again as well as the previous five paragraphs and think about how you have been bonding and then consider ways you might respond better for the sake of building an improved relationship. Work on adding excitement and fun to your marriage. Enjoy those touches, kisses and hugs and cuddling times together. Feel secure and loved in those acts rather than annoyed and your response will encourage the other and who knows how much closer you will feel in your relationship. That sounds like a couple falling in love again. You might find that you actually enjoy it.

Chapter Five: The Ultimate Goal is to Value Each Other

Sue thinks that if she and Ed could just connect emotionally more often and talk more frequently about what is on his mind, as well as have him listen to her attentively, then their relationship would get better. Ed thinks that if Sue would be more responsive and even show him love more often by initiating sex that would make their relationship better. What do you dream about the other person doing in your relationship that would improve everything? How do you bridge the gap so you will not only feel closer but also be more fulfilled? Do you ever ask yourself how you can make the other feel more fulfilled? What kind of steps and actions can help you move from dreaming to reality, from disappointment to fulfillment?

Ed and Sue is a strong willed couple. Sue doesn't want to give in to Ed unless she knows that Ed is going to properly respond to her. She has a stubborn streak and finds herself saying in her mind, "Well, I'm not going to meet his needs until he meets my needs." The problem is that many times he can't just "will himself" to open up, he needs that release of vasopressin and oxytocin that allows him to share freely. You are the key to it. Your relationship with him is very important and when you value that area of his life, he will, more than likely, take care of your need of communication. I'll say it again: "As good communication and emotional connection can open a woman to sex, so sex can open a man to good communication." In the way good sex can release men from the negative effects of cortisol so meaningful conversation and emotional connection plays a part in releasing a woman from the harmful effects of cortisol.

When we know how each functions we are more likely to meet their needs. It is easier to hit a visible target in the light than one that is concealed in darkness. Too many couples are shooting blindly at a target they can't see and therefore are missing the mark in their relationship. When you know how the other functions you will find that it increases the light shed on your target. The more light that is shed on the target of having a fulfilling relationship the better will be your odds of hitting it in the way you treat one another.

Learn to meet each other's needs, because that is what love is about. Love is willing to sacrifice for the benefit of the other and for the sake of the relationship. Love believes the best about the other and always seeks their betterment. Love is a commitment of your will to act on behalf of their highest need. When there is real love in the relationship sacrifice makes the relationship stronger because you are willing to serve their needs. That doesn't make you a slave to them, but it creates devotion to one another. When love is done right you seldom see the one taking advantage of the other.

Putting it into Practice

I hope this has been an enlightening journey into understanding your spouse more fully. The better we understand our mate's needs the easier it is to take them seriously. We relate best when we have a fuller understanding of the other. The purpose of this book has been to help open your eyes to important truths that drive the other as well as yourself. Such knowledge is not designed for you to learn how to take advantage of them, but to enlighten you in how to fulfill them in the way marriage was intended.

When the other is not meeting your need, it is easy to mount your high horse and say that you won't respond to the other person properly until they first respond properly to you. Who should initiate the first move to make things right? In our self centeredness we like to think that if the other person would take responsibility for their wrong action or responses we will then reciprocate and do what is right by them. We avoid personal vulnerability when we take the firm stand within our being that they must make the first move and then we will do right by them. But, is that the right response? What should you do?

I like what nationally known speaker on relationships, Emerson Eggerichs says about who should move first when neither is doing right. **"The one who is most mature should move first."** Will you accept the responsibility to move first or are you going to defer to the other? Don't let this be a Mexican standoff, because all that does is kill a relationship. Showing a mature love will cause you to make the first move. Don't let pride prevent you from making the best of your relationship.

Perhaps when you were kids at home there was sibling rivalry and one tried to best the other, get the most, or outwit the other. Competition is very common among children in a family when they feel they have to vie for attention. You are now adults and this is not a competition but a relationship in which each of you is devoted to the other. It is sad to see couples engage in sibling rivalry where they are fighting all the time and vying for attention to become the favorite, or seeking to be the best or do what they can to get the most. Their view of their relationship has failed to grow up and mature. They are treating their spouse in the same way they treated their siblings before they left home. They have remained locked into childish behavior and competition. Be a mature couple who aren't competing with each other, but valuing one another and working together to make the most of your relationship. Sometimes it's hard to get the child to grow up, even when they are married.

Become an MSI

How important is your relationship to you? It is sad that couples don't explore why they have negative feelings with one another in these areas of communication and sex. Once established in the relationship our attitudes seem to run along a certain course that closes the door to exploring why the other acts and reacts to our needs like they do. We are stuck in a rut and make little or no effort to get out so we can blaze a new trail. I've heard a rut is defined as a grave with open ends. To live, you need to get out of the grave and blaze a new trail into understanding and enlightenment about your relationship.

The next time you are offended or the other responds with anger or frustration to you, or your needs are not being met, take time during the next day and look objectively at the way you responded or treated the other. The **CSI** programs on television have been a big hit over the past decades and have taught people how to look at a crime scene objectively by considering the evidence and talking through the problem with other experts.

Why not become an **MSI**, a **M**arriage **S**cene **I**nvestigator, and learn to look at your relationship objectively rather than subjectively or emotionally. A **C**rime **S**cene **I**nvestigator does not get emotionally involved in the case but is able to look objectively at both the evidence and the problems so they can come to a reasonable conclusion. As an **MSI** you will learn to decode what the other person was really saying and find out what they actually meant. Think about what you could have said differently. Talk to experts, such as, mature couples who have a good working relationship or, if need be your pastor or a marriage counselor. Ask yourself meaningful

74

questions that will help you explore why you or the other is acting or reacting that way. Seek to understand the other and yourself. Here are some questions a **M**arriage **S**cene **I**nvestigator could ask:

a. Could you have done something differently or treated them better?
b. If you replayed the confrontation in your mind, how did you come across?
c. Did you really understand their motive or need or did you misread them?
d. Ask them calmly the next day where they were coming from because you want to understand them from their perspective rather than your perceived perspective.
e. Ask them how you came across in the way you reacted or responded to the difference.
f. What could you have done to change the outcome of your discussion or encounter?
g. If they are truly a good-willed person, did you understand their heart or did you just think the worst of their motive?
h. How would you have responded better if you had thought the best of what they did or said?
i. Did you "go off" on them too quickly before hearing them out?
j. Did you ask them questions without negative emotions to find out what they truly meant or wanted?
k. Why did you deny their request or not take it seriously? How much do you think it hurt them?
l. What kind of response would have made this situation not turn the corner so intensely?
m. Seek out information by asking them directly, "What would a better response have looked like to you?" Plug into your request such things as the kind of information you want from him when he tells you what happened in his day, or how he needs you to respond when he makes advances to you, or how you want them to respond in a disagreement. Tell the other what a proper response looks like from your perspective. Be straight forward, bold, kind and considerate as you ask or respond to such an inquiry.
n. The next time the other brings up an unpleasant topic, refuse to respond emotionally to them at all, but be calm, listen to all of what they have to say, ask questions to clarify anything you don't understand, and repeat to them what you think they said to you. In that way you will know if you are on the same page with the other.

75

It is when the other thinks the worst of us that we walk away thinking they just don't understand us, nor do they seem to care. That leads to frustration and eventually to anger. When it happens again we react even more strongly and our words get sharper. What are you going to do to open up the communication to new levels so you can understand your differences and better comprehend their needs and gain a better working relationship? What are your plans of how you can be there for him to meet his sexual needs? What are your plans of how you can open up to meet more of her emotional and communication needs? Be a good **M**arriage **S**cene **I**nvestigator and get to the root of what is fracturing your communication or other problems in your marriage and then talk it out and look for ways to work it out. Be specific in how the other person can be there for you. If you can't figure out the specifics of your problem or bring it to a solution between the two of you, then there are a lot of good books on marriage, and good counselors who can help you work through your problem areas as I mentioned above.

The key component to relationship maturity

The key to learning and teaching is to have a positive and concerned attitude. On the other hand an attitude of superiority or contempt for your mate does nothing to the process of developing of your relationship. There are times to be negative because issues need to be addressed, but a consistent negative attitude is usually destructive. If you find that you are negative, start choosing to be positive with your comments. If you find it hard to do so, then it is because you are so used to looking at people and life through a negative filter rather than a positive one. The key to a positive attitude is to value the other and have an attitude of concern for them and your relationship. That positive attitude causes you to be a builder and encourager rather than a destroyer and discourager.

A store clerk who doesn't listen to your complaint tends to irritate you, but one that is concerned about your problem leaves you feeling better, even if they didn't resolve the problem to your satisfaction. Their attitude is what makes the difference. It's easy to have a good attitude at the beginning of your relationship but the longer you are with one another the more you expect and the less tolerant you may become and it shows in your attitude. Jesus taught: *"As you would like people to do to you, do exactly so to them."*[16] What kind of attitude do you want the other to have with you when they deal with sensitive issues in your relationship? Running roughshod over a person emotionally may get them to do what you want at the moment, but it doesn't build a good relationship. A key component to building a growing relationship is to have a positive attitude toward your mate in how you believe in them, respond to them and the way you talk with them.

Having a positive attitude is vital to a good relationship. It is the fertile soil that allows the person to grow and develop their potential. What happens to the self worth of a person when their mate is critical and constantly finding fault? It hinders personal growth as well as relationship growth. How can you draw close to a person who is critical of you? This person presents themselves as one who doesn't believe in you, value you, see the best in you, or seek to understand your motives. It feeds depression, stifles creativity and is a wet blanket to their imagination. Their negativity tends to prey on you by building up themselves at your expense.

Is your relationship positive or is there a lot of criticism? Does it seem like one of you can't do anything right, or can you both feel comfortable even when you make a mistake? Does one of you often find ways to put the other down with pointed humor or sarcasm, and then hide behind cover up statements such as: "I was joking. Can't you take a joke?" Veiled comments put up walls in a relationship. Praise, appreciation, positive attitudes and acceptance opens the door to intimacy and relationship growth.

In a recent lecture I heard the speaker talk about the power of negative words. She said that negative words are more powerful than positive words. We find it easier to remember the negative words others have spoken to us than the positive words. Some kids grow up remembering only the negative words of how stupid they are, or how incompetent they are or how ugly they are. No matter how much they improve and better themselves they still have those negative words nagging in their minds. Negative words can crush one's spirit, destroy their dreams, and color their outlook of people and decisions. When your mate has a tendency to speak negatively to you then their words can reinforce your personal negative thoughts and feelings. In a marriage relationship it is reported that it takes at least seven positive statements to nullify one careless negative comment. Choosing to act and speak in a positive manner with your spouse will have beneficial effects in your relationship

Whereas negative statements close a person down, positive statements tend to open them up to new thoughts and ideas. Positive comments encourage a person and build them up. To have a dream that you both share and work on also tends to draw you closer together. Do you need to be more positive toward your mate? It is an essential quality in creating an atmosphere of openness and the development of personal potential.

Teach your mate about yourself

I found a page of notes recently on which I wrote the following statements that I heard or read a few years ago. It said: *"It is the man's job to teach his wife to love with her body. It is the wife's job to teach her husband to love with his soul."* When you stay focused on your unfulfilled needs you will get frustrated and usually become upset. Move beyond thinking about how your own needs are not being met and become proactive and seek to give the other a better understand of yourself and your needs. Look not just for ways but also the right opportunity to help them understand you and then teach them how to meet your needs. What can you do to teach your mate how to meet your needs? What will you do to reciprocate in learning about the deepest needs of your mate? Such understanding cannot be demanded but must be graciously and tenderly taught and learned in a loving atmosphere. Pick the right moments to talk about your needs, never when you are frustrated or hurt. Love takes a lot of work and commitment because we must go beyond our self centered focus and learn to value the other by embracing who and what they are as a person. We can't assume that the deepest needs are understood by the other just because we have hinted at them or mentioned them on occasion without going into more detail.

When Ed and Sue read this they both hit their forehead with the heel of their hand and in unison said "Duh, why did we think about that? It was so obvious!"

Ed was excited and said, "We have sure gone through a lot of frustration and what was most needed for us is something that we never considered." Why did we avoid telling each other about our needs?

Sue was more excited by Ed's response. She never thought they would come to this kind of a breakthrough in understanding each other and making their relationship better.

78

Before Sue could get over the shock of Ed's response he went on and said, "I would like us to start talking about this, but I know it's going to take a while for it to all sink in, so I would like to suggest that we get away for a romantic week (by this he is showing her that she is really important to him). He went on to describe what he wanted in that weekend: "We can do some fun things together, because you know how active I am. I also want us to set aside a lot of time to talk about our needs openly so our relationship has a better chance to reach its potential. Before we leave I'd like us to jot down some of the things that we most want the other to know and think about how we will articulate our personal needs to the other."

At that Ed heard a thud. *"Sue! Sue! What's the matter?"* he said as he bent down to pick her up. Ed is focused on Sue, but as we slip away we want to thank them for their involvement in helping us come to a better understanding of ourselves. Thanks Susan and Edward.

Annual Marriage Review

Over the years as a pastor one of the things I did on occasion was to have my board review my work. I wanted to know what it was that I was doing well and what could be improved. I knew I needed an objective evaluation of my work and ministry. A review can be very helpful for progressing.

Then in the final years of ministry we merged with another church and I became an associate pastor and I also came under review and questions were asked about my work. I had to do a self-evaluation first and then the lead pastor reviewed it with me. It helped in understanding where I was and where I needed to improve.

Because marriage is long term it is easy to get stuck in a rut and keep doing the same things and responding in the same way without getting new results. So we just keep responding in destructive ways without looking for ways to improve and better meet the needs of our spouse. This is where an *Annual Marriage Review* can be helpful. Questions on this list focus on the topic of the book; communication and sex. Allow my list to be a suggested list for your first Annual Marriage Review. Add your own questions that address your specific needs. Do this individually or as a couple.

Not all questions will be relevant. Some people may find so many relevant questions they do not know where to start. Perhaps the list will make you feel overwhelmed. Don't let that prevent you from doing your evaluation. Mark off the ones that are relevant. Reread the list again but this time pick no more than three areas to work on in the next few months. When you have become proficient with these then come back and choose a few more. It's not a race; it's more like a marathon. Actually it's not even a marathon; it is a life time relationship that you are working on.

You will find that as you work on some of the most significant questions that others may no longer be as relevant. If you are afraid to address some of these, then start with this easy one. *Look for specific actions and attitudes in their life for which to thank and praise them.* Don't ever give praise as an ulterior motive. Let it be sincere and from the heart. Are you ready to start?

Communication

a. Am I allowing the other to speak their mind on a topic without interruption?

b. Am I listening to what they have to say or do I cut them off and think I know what they want?

c. Do I seek to understand their need from their perspective or have I already made up my mine?

d. Do I think I am always right? If so, why is that so important?

e. Do I admit when I am wrong?

f. What do I fear about admitting when I am wrong?

g. When is the last time I admitted I was wrong and sincerely apologized?

h. Am I guilty of name-calling in an argument?

i. Do I listen and give full attention to the other or does my mind usually wonder to other things?

j. Am I consistently kind, thoughtful, honest, gracious and considerate in my conversations? What about in disagreements.

My attitude

a. Do I usually think the best or the worst of the other when they seem offensive to me? (Thinking the worst means that I think they have hostile intentions toward me.)

b. Do I listen completely and think for a few moments before answering or do I fly off the handle?

c. Am I reacting or responding to them? Why are you reacting?

d. What gives me the right to abandon rational thinking for undue emotion in my response?

e. Do I take on an attitude of superiority when in a disagreement?

f. I will do something good and that they enjoy spontaneously more often.

Sex

For the husband --

a. Do I get angry when she refuses me?

b. How do I feel when she refuses me? Is her response an accurate description of her true devotion to me?

c. Do I really think she ought to respond to have sex every time I make a request? Does she have a right to say no at that time without a negative response from me?

d. Do I think it is out of line to explain my needs to her?

e. When is the last time you talked with your wife about how often you need sex during a week?

f. When is the last time you talked with your wife about what she needs from you to prepare her for a good evening of sex?

g. If you need five seconds to be ready for sex, how long do you think your wife needs?

h. What is really important to your wife in preparing for sex?

For the wife --

a. How does my husband read my refusal to have sex when he asks?

b. Have you asked your husband how he feels when you refuse sex?

c. Have I honestly told my husband what I need to prepare for sex?

d. Have I told my husband what my turn-ons are?

e. Have I told my husband why I am often slow to be turned on or want sex?

f. Think about this in explaining your prep time for sex: *Your husband is like fireworks. He is ready to go quickly and he is done in a flash. You are more like a simmering pot of chili. It may take all day to cook, but when properly prepared you can be hot and spicy! When it is ready to eat it is not to be eaten quickly but enjoyed slowly and the flavor savored.*

g. If your husband needed sex three times a week, which days would you tell him that you will be available? How many times each week are you willing to have sex with your man?

Time together

a. How many times are we going to date a month?

b. Are you willing to plan half the dates if the other plans the other half?

c. Each should list ten activities they would like to do together during the coming year. Which of those things would please him? Which would please her?

d. Plan one week-end get away for just the two of you. (Make reservations, sitters for the kids and plan the events, even if it is just quiet time and sleeping in.) Surprises getaways are nice but talking about the getaway several weeks before creates an anticipation that is half the fun.

e. What would I like us to do for family vacation this year?

f. Have we been maintaining friendships with other couples?

Getting to know you talks

a. Does my mate feel safe in talking about hurts of the past or current disagreements?

b. Have I ever asked about my spouse's childhood trauma, hurts and disappointments? When they open up, give them freedom to talk uninterrupted with as much detail as they want. Don't judge them. Ask about the feelings they had during that time. Let them cry and don't feel like you have to stop them from crying because those tears are healing. What they tell you stays between the two of you if that's what they want.

c. Ask your spouse how they felt you treated them in the most recent argument. Allow them to express their feelings openly and freely. Don't be judgmental of them. Don't offer excuses or justification for your actions. Think about what they said for at least an hour before you respond. Thank them for sharing, for they have just shared information that will help make your relationship stronger.

d. When is the last time I held my spouse after they came home hurt or when a loved one died?

e. Do I think that my spouse feels more secure when they are being held?

f. Am I able to give non-sexual touches to connect with my spouse?

g. Have I opened up about my hurts from the past? What would make me feel safe in sharing some of the following feelings? What didn't my parents do that I wished they had? How would I have liked for them to treat me? How did they disappoint or hurt me?

h. Have I ever thought about setting ground rules for talking about past hurts with my spouse?

i. Why is it important to talk about hurts of the past? (Let me illustrate the importance of talking about past. In two minutes list at least four hurts you had as a child that you still remember. Did you have so many you wondered which ones to pick? Why do you still remember them? Because they made an emotional impact on your life and they are still fresh because they are wounds that have not yet healed.) Talking out your hurts cleanses the wound so healing can begin.

j. When is the last time I talked about my dreams with my spouse? How about our dreams?

k. Can I have a growing relationship or open communication if I am unwilling to forgive. What are indications that I am not forgiving? (Example: bitterness, anger touchiness, etc.) I will forgive them now for the grudges I have against them.

l. When and/or where is the best time I like to communicate and have good talks? Establish a plan for a time and place to go for uninterrupted communication.

m. Have I taken time to notice what the other has done and thank or praise them for it? I commit myself to do this every week.

The Journey of Understanding

It is interesting to watch a young couple in love. They can be so expressive of the love and desire to get to know the other. They are playful, they laugh a lot, they like to hold hands and kiss, and they talk about everything. Whenever they are together it is like watching an adventure of where they are genuine in their discovery and wonder.

Where did you lose the joy of "discovery and wonder" in your relationship? Why is the relationship not as exciting as it was before? After all you should still be getting to know each other and experiencing the best of life together. It was when you stopped paying attention to the other that life became routine.

You now come to the final phase of moving further into the adventure of your relationship. Meeting the needs of the one you love has to have a priority in your personal motivation. You will begin to move forward when you understand the needs of your spouse and consciously seek to, not just meet those needs, but to enjoy the process and learn to engage more vigorous in fulfilling their needs because you love them. When someone goes out of their way for you, do you tend to despise them or respect them? A relationship built on such understanding and effort builds a good relationship that produces abundant love, joy and peace in your journey as you travel through the valley and mountain top experiences of life together.

Do you understand your woman?
Do you understand your man?

May your relationship be a growing one that brings you contentment, excitement and mutual fulfillment. May you both enjoy a lot of hot sex and satisfying conversation in your growing relationship.

Addendum 1

Cortisol and Oxytocin

In seeking to understand the effects of Oxytocin and Vasopressin I went to several websites. I share here some of the findings I discovered because some people want to know more detail. In the book I only use brief quotes from lengthy articles, so if you want more information check it out for yourself. This is not my area of expertise but is placed here to give you fuller understanding of the topic and how it affects a person. Keep in mind that science is in the early stages of their research and there will be much more to discover.

"Oxytocin is a powerful hormone released by men and women during orgasm. It is released into the brain of the male and female during sexual activity and is important for forming a bond with their sexual partner." Oxytocin released in the brain under stress-free conditions naturally promotes sleep, according to a 2003 study in the Journal Regulatory Peptides. (http://poundpuplegacy.org/node/48416) Ellison said this link makes sense because oxytocin counters the effects of cortisol, which is known as the stress hormone. "It has a calming effect," she said. "It leaves you feeling tranquil and loving, and certainly that helps our path to sleep."

In another article it said: "Oxytocin causes your brain to react less fearfully, less anxiously than it normally would. Stress is reduced and you feel more content. Oxytocin also makes people more trusting and more understanding of others." (http://www.giusisilvestri.com/articles/how-women-differ-to-men/)

Oxytocin is a hormone that women need both to have and to enjoy sex. In fact it gives women a feeling of satisfaction. Optimal levels of oxytocin for a woman actually result in lowering her stress level and as a result give her more energy and the ability to climax or feel sexually satisfied after sex. One way to increase a woman's oxytocin level is to engage in sex, because oxytocin is produced by sexual arousal and orgasm. Vasopressin is another hormone that appears to have a similar calming effect in males. It is an important hormone in the long-term commitment stage and is released after sex.

In the above paragraph it is stated that oxytocin is needed in women to have and enjoy sex. Perhaps this indicates that women need and enjoy the time of preparing for sex. The meaningful conversation, emotional attachment, good humor, the wooing and taking personal interest in her helps the production of oxytocin that prepares her to enjoy it, and then when she climaxes there is even a greater release of oxytocin which leads to greater bonding and attachment.

Men like this statement. "Oxytocin probably deepens the feelings of attachment and makes couples feel much closer to one another after they have had sex. The theory goes that the more sex a couple has, the deeper their bond becomes." http://www.youramazingbrain.org.uk/lovesex/sciencelove.htm)

Is cortisol good hormones or bad hormones? These hormones are often characterized as being bad hormones, but they are also essential for life. In the correct range, cortisol, promotes proper function of the brain.

More Cortisol is secreted in stressful conditions of life. In excessive amounts it can have a negative effect. Examples of Chronic Stress Related Diseases are: Coronary heart disease, hypertension, tension headaches, post-traumatic stress syndrome, stroke, **depression**, backache, fatigue, and lethargy, autoimmune diseases, insomnia, asthma, overeating, ulcer, frigidity.

Effects of Cortisol: Decreases the effects of insulin on blood glucose, Increases blood glucose, Increases fat and cholesterol in the blood, Increases breakdown of proteins into amino acids, decreases inflammation, immune system function, and healing, decreases memory. (http://wellness.byu.edu/pics/documents/stress-revised%20-%20handouts%20(2).pdf)

Stress Reducers

People who see the humor in day to day life and the humor associated with stressful situations handle stress better than those that take life overly seriously. Therefore, "lighten up". Good relationships with family and others help in the management of stress. The feeling of belonging is also very important. If you react emotionally and keep everyone hyped up by your sarcasm, snide comments, yelling, negative reactions to life, you need to think about making some serious attitude changes so you can have more of a positive influence in your relationship. Don't justify such actions.

When cortisol is prominent it can have negative effects on your brain. When oxytocin is released there are positive effects in your life. Sex is one of the stimulations for the secretion of oxytocin in your brain. As mentioned above we notice that humor as well as good relationships with your spouse and the feeling of belonging also produces oxytocin. Here are negatives effects of cortisol followed by the positive effects of oxytocin.

Fear – Cortisol

a. Aggression
b. Arousal, Anxiety, Feeling stressed-out
c. Activates addictions
d. Suppresses libido
e. Associated with depression
f. Can be toxic to brain cells
g. Breaks down muscles, bones and joints
h. Weakens immune system
i. Increases pain
j. Clogs arteries, promotes heart disease and high blood pressure

Love - Oxytocin

a. Anti-stress hormone
b. Feeling calm and connected, increased curiosity
c. Lessens cravings & addictions
d. Increases sexual receptivity
e. Positive feelings
f. Facilitates learning
g. Repairs, heals and restores
h. Faster wound healing
i. Diminishes sense of pain
j. Lowers blood pressure, protects against heart disease

(http://www.reuniting.info/science/sex_and_addiction)

The following expresses some of the other ways oxytocin is produced as well as describing the added benefits of oxytocin.

a. Frequent hugs between partners associated with lower blood pressure and more oxytocin
b. Touch and psychological support are health-promoting due to increased oxytocin
c. Oxytocin strongly protects organs from damage due to blood infection
d. Kissing may have positive implications for allergic patients
e. Oxytocin speeds wound healing and reduces pain
f. Oxytocin counters addiction and soothes withdrawal symptoms
g. Massage aids detoxification for alcohol, oxytocin rises during massage
h. Oxytocin reduces anxiety and stress
i. Less oxytocin results in more aggression and less caring
j. Oxytocin regulates cell proliferation and inhibits breast and prostate cancer
k. Oxytocin increases the receptivity of females
l. Oxytocin involved in learning and memory

Quoted from: HEALING WITH SEXUAL ENERGY. Sex for Health, Relationships and Spirituality; By Walter Last. (http://www.health-science-spirit.com/healsex.html)

Addendum 2

When I started writing on this topic my goal was to have a four page paper I could share with people. My reason for having it that length was because many people just are not readers. They will read a short article, but they won't read a longer book. As I worked on this project it went from a paper to a book.

Perhaps as you have read this book you realize that someone who could benefit from this book might be more inclined to read a shorter paper. So I am including the material from my original paper here to share with those in your life who will benefit from an overview of the book.

"Communication and Sex" Abridged Version

Do conversation and sex have something in common?

What do conversation and sex have in common? Both are important to developing a good marriage relationship. To understand this, one must understand what both of them accomplish in a man and a woman. Understanding the teachings of this book can help negate bitter feelings and frustration you may feel when your basic needs are not met by the other.

When it comes to sex, it has been said that women are like crock-pots and men are like microwave ovens. Men are ready to engage at a moment's notice. Women need time to be wooed. Communication is foreplay for the woman. Visual stimulation, thoughts and touch, and not always very much of it, can make a man ready to engage sex. The differences are obvious and often joked about.

So what is it that communication and sex have in common? The answer is, they both accomplish the same thing when carried out. Does that have you guessing even more? I hope so, because it is imperative that each one in the relationship understands what these accomplish for the other.

Women and Communication

Women are about relationship. They want to cultivate and nurture relationship. This is their motivation behind talking and communication.

Communication is about passing on information. That is why, when you come home, she wants to share the experiences of her day so you know what went on and in this way you can connect with her. She will share not only what happened but also her opinions and feelings about what happened. Men may become annoyed with trivial information at times, because they don't understand why she has to include all that detail.

When she asks her husband what happened in his day then she wants him to share the significant details of his day so she can understand what he went through and how he felt. However, the man has another view of the details of the day. If he worked through a problem with the job or a person and brings it to a resolution, he is finished with it. It is over. What good does it do to rehash it? So he doesn't understand why that is so important to her to know what happened. He doesn't "get it" that such details help her connect with him and feel closer. It fulfills an important need in her life for connection.

When she asks you why you are so late, or why didn't you call she wants to know what tied you up, if you had any problems or are we having a problem? Oft times he reads this kind of "inquisition" as her being his parent or being over protective, or being on his case.

But the motivation is so she can know what is going on in your life. She wants to be there for you, to be a part of your life. Her desire is to connect with you because that is what relationship is all about. When you misread her motivation and respond with snide comments, then you attack the core of her being. She wants to connect with you and to be a part of your life. It's important that you de-code what she is really saying. That becomes difficult for you when she uses a tone of voice that sounds more accusative rather than concerned.

When she wants to get away from everything in a romantic evening, her motivation is to have new experiences, to connect by talking about things that are important to the both of you and to not be distracted by the common things of life. She wants to connect with you because that is her most important need. When you take her to places she likes without having been told, or you buy her gifts that you "know" she will like, then that is telling her that she has connected with you in relationship. She wants you to attend to her needs and be aware of the relationship you have with her.

When she feels you are connected with her, knows that you value her, and has her needs met, then typically, physical intimacy is her expression in which she gives herself to you fully. You could say that a woman is like dynamite with a long fuse. The fuse has to be lit through communication and sharing life events, thoughts, concerns, feelings. This can go on for a while, but the result is that there will be sexual explosion. Her sexual expression comes from her needs being met through communication in its many forms. This is very important for men to know. It is something that many women don't fully understand either.

Men and Sex

Have you ever wondered why a couple can be angry with each other, not getting along and then after they have sex the man thinks everything is all right and the problems have been settled? It just doesn't make sense. Nothing has been resolved, nothing has been discussed, all he's done is had sex. There is no communication in the sex. No exchange of information. Yet the man feels absolutely fulfilled. What's going on here? Does the man have no soul? Is he just about the physical?

A woman has a hard time relating to what motivates a man in the area of sex. He wants to touch her (intimately) and sometimes for no reason at all. She wonders if she is just a sexual object to fulfill his needs, and what needs are really being met? Are men just animals in their desires, doing it for the sake of doing it? She sees nothing being accomplished with those touches or those "quickies". Often sex for her is a response to satisfy him, but it has no real significant meaning, not like it has to him. It's often just one more annoyance in her life. After all, everything gets accomplished through good communication. She just doesn't get it with her husband. They are so different. Will they ever get anywhere if he doesn't learn to communicate?

Let me say this, even though the wife deeply loves her husband and is willing to meet his sexual needs, most women don't understand what sex accomplishes for the man. The fact of the matter is that neither does he. That is why this teaching is so important and must be understood. If a woman wants that deep intimacy with him, then she needs to realize that she must communicate in two languages: male and female. To not think that you need to understand male communication leads to trouble. Men and women do not think alike.

Dennis Rainey comments on this truth: *"When a man is rejected often enough, he typically internalizes his anger, his hurt, and his disappointment until such time when the rejection drives him to one of several reactions— none of them are good. He will give up on the relationship, he will seek alternative sexual outlets such as pornography, or he might compromise his wedding vows by pursuing female affirmation elsewhere."*

The Path to Fulfillment

The woman feels connected when there is communication and sharing of thoughts, events, concerns, fears and dreams. That touches the heart of her being. When this is accomplished she feels connected to her man. A man can appreciate this and can come to enjoy it and it can mean a lot to him. But it does not touch his soul and bring him fulfillment like it does to the woman. Sex touches the soul of a man and gives him fulfillment.

--What communication is to a woman, sex is to a man.
--The way communication fulfills a woman, sex fulfills a man.
--The way communications attracts the soul of a woman, sex attracts the soul of a man.
--The way in which a man and a woman are fulfilled are different and must be respected.

Did I say it in enough different ways that you got it? This does not mean that a man doesn't enjoy communication nor does it mean that women don't enjoy sex. It's just saying that they accomplish different things for men and women.

So when men touch (or as you might call grope), when they have sex, whether it seems like it couldn't really have been a meaningful experience or not, the fact remains sex touches his soul. It makes him feel connected to you. It is the same kind of connection you feel with him when you have meaningful communication. The result of feeling connected may or may not bring on an openness of sharing, but it does make him feel connected to you as well as fulfilled.

When you start talking with your husband and he cuts you off and makes you think what you have to share is unimportant, what does that do to you? Does it make you feel frustrated, upset or angry? It probably makes you feel like you are not important or significant to him? He has cut off that which is so valuable in developing and maintaining relationship. You are hurt. How do you respond? Will you say: "If he doesn't value me then why should I value him?" The problem is that neither the man nor woman usually understands how they reject their spouse, or how much they hurt their spouse by their rejection.

It is imperative to the relationship that he understands the importance of communication to you and what it accomplishes. Sometimes it is not enough to just talk, but take the opportunity to teach him why it is important that he listen to you. You may have to choose the right times to share. Have a time set aside each evening where you can share the events of the day and how you feel about them, or talk about urgent issues.

Don't dump on him as soon as he enters the door after work. Give him time to catch his thoughts and rest a bit. Talk about the importance of this time and agree on a regular time to set aside specifically for this communication. It might be something as simple as having no TV or distraction so you can talk over dinner.

When he approaches you sexually and you cut him off or push him away, he experiences the very same kind of feelings of rejection you feel when he doesn't want to listen to you. He feels that he is not really that important to you. He has the very same kind of feelings of rejection that you had when he wouldn't talk or let you talk, he also feels rejected when you push him away or put him off and not treat his need for sex as important. His rejection and feeling of abandonment is just as real as yours when he didn't see the importance of talking with you.

You are both alike in your responses

Just like most women don't fully know why they need to communicate with their husbands so most husbands don't understand why sex is so important to them. You both just know what is important.

Communication and sex give us connection and fulfillment in the relationship with the person we love dearly. It's now time for you to understand that truth and take it seriously in your relationship. It's just as important for the man to value the wife's need for communication as it is for the wife to value the man's need for sex in the relationship.

So if you want to have a relationship in which she is more willing to meet your needs she needs to hear from you about what is going on in your day and she needs you to listen and be concerned about what happened in her life. It may not be easy for you because it is not natural, but it is something you need to learn and do. Just as responding to you for sex all the time is not always natural or easy for her, but she needs to understand your needs and how it affects you.

When she has had a stressful day she wants to unload right away. Everything is running rampant in her mind and then you come in she wants to tell you everything. That is how she deals with stresses, lingering thoughts and concerns in life. She has to express her thoughts or she will get even more frustrated. She has to share them with the man she loves. Do you understand how that plays out?

When it comes to sex the man is very visual and the thought of sex comes easily to his mind. He thinks about it, and wants it, and he can imagine being with you and being close to you. How do you think he feels when he approaches you and you don't take him very seriously, or dismiss his desires as unimportant or childish? Just as you get frustrated with him when he doesn't want to listen and talk, so he also gets equally frustrated and even angry because you rejected him. Many times when he rolls over because of your rejection of him, that hurt can turn into anger or frustration. Just like you feel when he has not responded to your needs.

For a woman SEX is spelled C-h-o-c-o-l-a-t-e

Nancy Anderson does a nice job of explaining a man's sexual needs in a way that women understand. She said: *"Ladies, have you ever gone on a PMS-driven mission called "Gotta have chocolate, or someone's gonna die"? I have. I once ransacked every drawer in my son's room looking for last year's semi-sweet Easter Bunny's ear. I've clawed through the kitchen cupboards like Indiana-Jones on a quest, looking for a little golden bag containing stale chocolate chips. As I ripped it open and blissfully inhaled the aroma, my pulse reacted as if I'd just found the necklace that the old lady threw off the Titanic.*

Now imagine that you're on a take-no-prisoners chocolate chase and your husband has a Snickers bar in his locked briefcase—but he won't give you the key. He has the capability to relieve your hormonal obsession, but he refuses. How would you feel about him? Would you think that he was selfish? Mean? Cruel? That's how a man feels when his wife rejects his sexual needs."

Conclusion

It is easier to take someone's needs more seriously when we know what it is and why this need is so important. The purpose of this book has been to help open your eyes to this important truth.

It is easy to say that you won't respond to the other person properly until they respond properly to you. Who should make the first move to make sure things are done right? In our self centeredness we like to think it is the other person's responsibility and then we will respond when they make the first move. I like what Emerson Eggerichs says about who should move first when neither are doing right. The one who is most mature should move first. Don't let this be a Mexican Standoff, because all that does is kill a relationship. Be mature in your actions and response.

Good relationship has to do with understanding the needs of the other and consciously seeking to, not just meet those needs, but to enjoy the process and learn to appreciate the expression of those needs because you love them. Out of such understanding comes good relationship. Do you understand your woman? Do you understand your man? May your relationship be a growing one that brings excitement and fulfillment.

Other Kindle Books by James Olah

What is the Tone of Your Communication?

How does tone of voice affect your communication? How tone changes your message or enhances your words: Guidelines for dealing with communication problems in relationships.

This book addresses how tone of voice affects the way you communicate. Many sabotage their relationship, not because of the words they speak but the way they speak their words. You can have the best intentions and love the other dearly, but the way your words come out can kill the spirit of the other, get them frustrated or angry ready to defend their self from what they perceive is an attack or fight to protect their honor. This eye opening book will help you to not just see yourself but hear yourself better when you are talking with your loved one. Insightful questions and practical suggestions are offered in a thoughtful way to help you work through the problem areas. If you don't think you need this book, read it so you understand those around you who do have a problem with the way they use their tone of voice.

Kindle Books: ASIN B004Y020KU

"Getting to Know You": Questions to help prepare for marriage

This is a book of more than 300 questions that help you focus on many different areas important for a good relationship. It gives you the tough questions you need to ask yourself about the other person. One of the problems couples have is that they don't spend enough time getting to know what the other thinks about their beliefs and views of life. The more surprises you uncover before marriage and talk out ahead of time the stronger your marriage can be.

This book is one that parents will want to get for their teen or young adult children to help them understand some of the important issues of the makeup of a good relationship.

This book is designed to direct your thinking process for getting to know that special person. Do you really know the person that you are thinking of marrying? Do you know the kind of tough questions you need to ask?

This book of questions will assist you in your quest to gain understanding of that person who may become your life partner in marriage.

This book is made up of comments, observations and questions to guide you in your process of thinking realistically as you seek to get to know another person.

This book asks both the easy and difficult questions that help you reveal yourself to that special person and assist them in disclosing who they really are.

This book is not only important for those not yet married but can be valuable for those who are married.

This book is a wealth of common sense questions that can help you avoid conflict in the years ahead.

This book offers several practical and informative helps in the supplemental section for those who are getting married as well as for the newly married. Topics include understanding the other's world view, date night, setting goals, celebrating holidays, how to do a marriage tune up, and considerations for those who cohabitate.

Kindle Books: ASIN: B003VTZW71

Check out my author page for other books:
http://www.amazon.com/James-Olah/e/B005WLXP5O

End Notes

[1] From THE FEMALE BRAIN by Luanne Brizendine M.D. Page 82. Published by Broadway Books a division of Random House. Copyright 2006.

[2] *See author's Amazon Kindle book -B004Y020KU "WHAT IS THE TONE OF YOUR COMMUNICATION?" Description of book is above.*

[3] Excerpt from FOR WOMEN ONLY, REVISED AND UPDATED EDITION: WHAT YOU NEED TO KNOW ABOUT THE INNER LIVES OF MEN by Shaunti Feldhahn, copyright © 2004, 2013 by Veritas Enterprises, Inc. Used by permission of WaterBrook Multnomah, an imprint of the Crown
Publishing Group, a division of Random House LLC. All rights reserved. Any third party use of this material, outside of this publication, is prohibited. Interested parties must apply directly to Random House LLC for permission.

[4] **NO MORE HEADACHES**, Enjoying Sex and Intimacy in Marriage" by Dr. Juli Slattery. Pages 102-109. Copyright 2009 A Focus on the Family book published by Tyndale House Publication, Inc. Carol Stream, Illinois 60188.

[5] Excerpted from **"Five Keys to Your Man's Inner Heart"** by Dennis Rainey. Copyright © 2003 FamilyLife. Used by Permission. All Rights Reserved. **www.FamilyLife.com**

[6] The Flint Journal – Sunday, July 31, 2011

[7] "Seven Ways to Woo a Woman Properly" by Virginia B Gaces September 27, 2008 Found at: http://socyberty.com/men/seven-ways-to-woo-a-woman-properly/

[8] From EVERY MAN'S BATTLE (Every man's guide to winning the war on sexual temptation one Victory at a Time.) By: Stephen Arterburn and Fred Stoeker with Mike Yorkey. Published by Waterbrook Press. P. 63-64

[9] Nancy C. Anderson "Avoiding the Greener Grass Syndrome" Kregel 2004. Used by permission.
http://www.positivelyfeminine.org/relationships/marriage/na/monster.htm

[10] Source: Ten Important Research Findings on Marriage and Choosing a Marriage Partner -Helpful Facts for Young Adults- By: David Popenoe and Barbara Dafoe Whitehead at The National Marriage Project. Source: http://http://www.virginia.edu/marriageproject/pdfs/pubTenThingsYoungAdults.pdf Used by permission.

[11] Mary Whelchel "Dealing with Loneliness" © 2011 The Christian Working Woman - P.O. Box 1210, Wheaton, IL 60187-1210 -

http://www.christianworkingwoman.org/dealing_loneliness

[12] OF MICE AND MEN by John Steinbeck Copyright John Steinbeck, 1937. Copyright renewed by John Steinbeck, 1965. Published by arrangement with Viking Penguin, a division of Penguin Books USA Inc. pg. 72

[13] From WORLD ENGLISH BIBLE, (WEB). The WORLD ENGLISH BIBLE is in the public Domain and is part of the Online Bible. (http://www.onlinebible.net/)

[14] From THE FEMALE BRAIN by Luanne Brizendine M.D. Page 72. Published by Broadway Books a division of Random House. Published 2006. For online information about other Random House, Inc. books and authors, see the Internet web site at http://www.randomhouse.com

[15] From THE FEMALE BRAIN by Luanne Brizendine M.D. Page 68. Published by Broadway Books a division of Random House. Published 2006. "From an experiment on hugging, we also know that oxytocin is naturally released in the brain after a twenty-second hug from a partner—sealing the bond between the huggers and triggering the brain's trust circuits." "Touching, gazing, positive emotional interaction, kissing, and sexual orgasm also release oxytocin in the female brain."

[16] Luke 6:31 WORLD ENGLISH BIBLE, (WEB). The WORLD ENGLISH BIBLE is in the public Domain and is part of the Online Bible. (http://www.onlinebible.net/)

Made in the USA
Charleston, SC
25 November 2013